The Moral World
of the First Christians

Library of Early Christianity

Wayne A. Meeks, General Editor

The Moral World
of the First Christians

Wayne A. Meeks

The Westminster Press
Philadelphia

Book design by Gene Harris

First Edition

Published by The Westminster Press®
Philadelphia, Pennsylvania

PRINTED IN THE UNITED STATES OF AMERICA

9 8 7 6 5 4 3 2

**To Paul and Sally Sampley
and the world of Charlemont**

Library of Congress Cataloging-in-Publication Data

Meeks, Wayne A.
   The moral world of the first Christians.

   (Library of early Christianity ; v. 6)
   Bibliography: p.
   Includes index.
      1. Christian ethics—History—Early church, ca.
30–600.   2. Ethics, Ancient.   3. Ethics, Jewish—
History.   I. Title.   II. Series.
BJ1212.M44   1986   241′.0412   86-5504
ISBN 0-664-21910-1

Contents

Preface

I cannot begin to name all the people who have helped me write this book. Generations of students have put in their word, from an undergraduate seminar at Dartmouth in 1965 to a graduate seminar at Yale in 1984, and in many private conversations. During the writing, the ideas and questions of the following have been especially helpful: Larry Yarbrough, Tony Lewis, Alan Mitchell, David Dawson, Susan Garrett, Dale Martin, Sam Fleischacker, Don Westblade, Sally Purvis, and David Kuck.

If there are any ideas here which I did not sometime absorb from my colleagues, near or far, I'll be surprised. Abraham Malherbe receives special thanks, both for what he has taught me in many ways, including his companion volume in this series, and for his critical reading of chapter 2. Ramsay MacMullen, Gene Outka, Victor Furnish, and my wife, Martha, have carefully read the entire manuscript and made numerous suggestions for improvement. I thank them all and beg their indulgence for those few instances in which I remain unpersuaded. Finally, I am grateful to Keith Crim and the capable staff of The Westminster Press for making the Library of Early Christianity possible, and especially to Cynthia Thompson for her gentle firmness, her patience, and her good ideas.

Introduction

How shall we understand the ethics of the first Christians? Obviously there are many facts about them which we need to learn, but even more important than the facts are the questions that we ask. A fully historical understanding of ethics requires that we ask some questions about things that we usually do not think of as belonging to ethics at all.

For example, when the apostle Paul writes, "If any one is disposed to be contentious, we recognize no other practice, nor do the churches of God" (1 Cor. 11:16), we may feel that he has abandoned ethical argument (in this case his argument does not seem to have been working out well) and resorted to social pressure to get what he wants. And that, we feel, is not really ethics.

We tend to think of ethics as moral argument or rules. We live in a culture of experts, in which there are professional ethicists who are expert in the construction of arguments and the analysis of rules. The ethicists themselves are usually uncomfortable at our putting them in such a role, for they often say that ethics is not like a technical field in which specialized knowledge is required in order to make good decisions. Nevertheless, because the rules and arguments advanced by different people and groups often conflict, especially in our pluralist society, we find that we need experts to sort out the confusion for us. So, for example, even hospitals and corporations hire ethicists, to tell people how to make moral decisions. This is ethics from the top down.

There is, however, a way of looking at ethics from the bottom up, in which it is a perfectly proper form of ethical directive to say, for example to a child, "We do not do that." Probably the response from the child, and perhaps also from the professional ethicist, will be, "Why not?" Very often that is an important question to ask, but there are other occasions when it may be more productive to ask a different question: Who are "we"? The question "Why?" calls for an explanation; "Who?" invites understanding. In the following pages we will try to keep both kinds of questions together.

Most, perhaps all, of the writings that now make up the New Testament, and a great many of the other earliest Christian writings as well, had as their primary aim the shaping of the life of Christian communities. Arguments and rules, of course, had their place in those writings, but we fail to understand the force of the arguments and rules if we take them out of the contexts in which they stand. A much more comprehensive process was going on, by which participants in the new movement we call Christianity were discovering a new identity—learning to think of themselves as "the churches of God," "the holy ones," "children of God," "slaves of Christ," "brothers and sisters," "those for whom Christ died," and so on. "Practice" or "custom" (*synētheia,* the word which Paul used in the verse quoted above) was not something added to that process of developing identity, but an integral part of it. The writers repeatedly urge all the Christians to "exhort," "admonish," and "encourage" one another. The aim of such moral conversation is, as Paul puts it in another place, "that you should behave in a manner worthy of the God who calls you" (1 Thess. 2:12, my trans.).

The history of the early Christian movement can thus be written as the development of "communities of moral discourse," as they have been called.[1] Still better is Stanley Hauerwas's term, "communities of character,"[2] for more than talk contributes to the shaping of behavior, and "character" suggests the essential dialectic between community and self. Groups as well as individuals have character. Character signifies identity, and it implies specifically moral identity. Character takes shape, moreover, within a social process. In this book we will be trying to understand some particular dimensions of the social process by which the character of the Christian communities of the first two centuries took form.

The first Christian groups did not exist on islands or in deserts. They lived in villages or cities. In the villages, daily behavior was controlled by the routines of necessity, the cycles of seasonal labor in the fields, customs as old as the oldest memory. Identity was a matter of family and clan, and family honor was a powerful sanction affecting every choice. To act in a way that brought shame on one's family or on a prominent member of it was dreadful. Soon the new movement spread beyond the villages of Judea and Galilee. Within a few years, the majority of the Christian groups were to be found in the various cities around the eastern perimeter of the Mediterranean. There, to be sure, life was more diverse than in rural villages, and the ties of clan and custom less firm. Nevertheless, city life was crowded and public, gossip flew through neighborhoods, and the behavior of a new club or cult or superstition—however the Christians were perceived—was sure to be an object of curiosity. It was not only that the Christians, wherever they lived, were under certain pressures from without to conform to the patterns of the larger society. Those patterns were part of themselves, part of who they were, how they thought and how they felt.

Now it is true that to join the Christian movement entailed "conversion" or what some sociologists call "resocialization." That is, becoming a Christian was expected to affect some of the most fundamental relationships, values, perceptions of reality, and even structures of the self, which are acquired by a child in the process of growing up within the family. Thus the Christians could speak of their initiation variously as a dying and rising with Christ, as a second birth, as adoption into a new family of God's children. The radicality of the metaphors bespeaks a real experience of sharp displacement which many of the converts must have felt. Nevertheless, they are metaphors, and they overstate the case. One cannot ever completely efface or replace the primary socialization, and the Christians did not try to do so, even though some of the things they said may make us think they did. For example, Paul wrote, "Do not be conformed to this world, but be transformed by the renewal of your mind" (Rom. 12:2). Yet his typical admonitions, which follow those words, are sprinkled with topics and turns of phrase that would be instantly recognizable in the moral rhetoric of his time and place. The Christians whose moral formation we are trying to understand lived in the world of the early Roman empire, and that world also lived in them: in their thinking, in their language, in their relationships.

In order to understand the moral formation of the early Christian communities, therefore, we must understand their world. When we speak of "their world" or "the world of the Roman empire," however, we betray a sense of something very odd about the concept "world." On the one hand, nothing is more objective to us than our world; it is simply *there* and we must relate to it. Yet if we compare our description of that objective world with, say, a Bushman's description, or the description by a monk of thirteenth-century Europe, we are driven to the conclusion that different people may have different worlds. The differences are not absolute, of course; otherwise we could never hope to understand people from another time and place. Nevertheless, in some cases the differences are quite fundamental. This odd state of affairs—that the world which one society takes to be simply, undeniably factual may be taken by another society to be alien, quaint, or preposterous—comes about because the world in which we in fact live is a symbolized world. It is a world in which the sensations that pour in constantly upon us through our senses are organized and thus have meaning through a system of signs so much a part of us that we are rarely aware of them as such. Thus it is easy for us, most of the time, to dismiss the world of the Bushman or of the medieval monk as simply wrong, because it is so different from the one we *know.* Yet we learned our system; it was given to us as part of that same process by which we became self-conscious persons.[3]

Furthermore this symbolized, socially learned world in which I live obviously affects the way I behave. On a flat earth I will not sail west to get to the East Indies. If my world is one in which witches are known to thrive, then the onset of high fever, sore throat, and diarrhea may lead me to ask sharply which of my fellow villagers may have a grudge against me. I will consult the tribal expert for countermagic. In a "modern" society the same symptoms will cause me to suspect a viral infection, and I will consult a physician. If I move from, say, a rural part of Haiti to New York, I may be faced with a choice. Some of my fellow members of the immigrant Haitian community may still practice the methods that other New Yorkers will call "magic," while others in the same community will disdain such things as "primitive."

These latter reflections suggest that, under certain circumstances, the objectivity of our world, or at least parts of it, can be undermined. Worlds do change. Notice that the change of worlds means the change of symbols; it is a process of relearning. But since the world was first acquired as part of a larger process of socialization, its change involves a resocialization. We may change our way of perceiving the world because we change communities: we emigrate to another country, for example, or we convert to a sect. That "because," however, is more ambiguous than we might think, for it is not always easy to say which comes first, the social change or the symbolic change. I may emigrate or convert because the world of the other community has come to seem truer to me than that of my former society. Or I may be forced into the new setting and only gradually come to understand and adopt its world view. In most cases both sorts of changes go on simultaneously, in a sort of dialectic.

As we endeavor to understand the moral formation of the early Christian communities, we begin by trying to understand the symbolic and social world they shared with other people in their villages or cities. Then we shall try to discover what kinds of resocialization and what changes of those symbolic worlds happened when people became Christians.

To emphasize the underlying, taken-for-granted patterns of the moral life, I will sometimes use the English word "ethos." Both "ethos" and "ethics" come from the Greek word *ēthos* (character). It was a cliché in Greek moral writing in antiquity, found already in Plato and Aristotle, that *ethos* led to *ēthos;* that is, "habit" (practicing the virtues until they became second nature) would eventually build "character." Because we are interested in tracing the development of "communities of character," that is still a pertinent observation. However, I am using "ethos" in a different way, suggested in the classic essay by the anthropologist Clifford Geertz, "Ethos, World View, and the Analysis of Sacred Symbols."[4] "A people's ethos," he writes, "is the tone, character, and quality of their life, its moral and aesthetic style and mood; it is the underlying attitude toward themselves and their world that life reflects." "Their world view," he continues, "is their picture of the way things in sheer actuality are, their concept of nature, of self, of society." From his fieldwork and the studies of other ethnographers, Geertz further concludes that religious symbols are connected with both world view and ethos, and indeed serve in virtually all societies to synthesize the two. "Such religious symbols, dramatized in rituals or related in myths, are felt somehow to sum up, for those for whom they are resonant, what is known about the way the world is, the quality of the emotional life it supports, and the way one ought to behave while in it." Geertz's triangle may help us to find our way through the complex picture of ancient society that will emerge in the following chapters.

There is one other insight shared by Geertz with a number of other anthropologists and philosophers which may help make clear the plan of this book. Culture, of which ethos, world view, and religious symbols are all parts, is an elaborate set of signs, a system of communication. Understanding culture—and so, understanding any of these parts—is like learning a language. Note: culture is *like* a language, but it is not identical with language. Language is the supreme and paradigmatic form of human communication, but not the only form. When Helen Keller grasped the connection between the word "water" spelled into her hand and the sensation of cold liquid flowing over the other hand, that epiphany of language was the decisive moment beginning her transformation into a social, articulate person. Yet it was not the first step. Her family and "the miracle worker" Anne Sullivan had already bombarded the three living senses she possessed with evidence that she was connected with a family, an order, a world of meaning. The symbolization of both feeling and meaning had already far advanced before the symbol "water" could be conceived. So gesture, form, arrangement, many things communicate and thus are part of the socializing and humanizing process. But language is the cap and epitome of culture.

Unfortunately all we have left from the Christian communities of the first two centuries is words. In this book I invite the reader to join me in an effort to piece together, in our imagination, what we can of the world within which those words once worked. We shall begin with an outline map that is broad in time and cultural boundaries, ranging from classical Greece four centuries before Christianity began down to the high Roman empire. We shall look in turn at the social worlds and the worlds of moral discourse of people within those boundaries.

Insofar as possible, I have tried not to summarize and generalize, but to lead the reader into a certain way of reading the available evidence. To make that reading easier, I have limited my attention to a select number of texts, both from the extra-Christian and from the Christian sources, and I have referred to them in translations that are readily available. The reader ought if possible to have these texts at hand. If this book is used in a course, assignments in the primary sources should accompany it. Moreover, the way of reading I propose does not require any special expertise, and the reader who arrives at conclusions different from mine should be unabashed.

Those who are familiar with other books on New Testament or early Christian ethics will miss in this one several familiar items. I do not have a chapter on "the ethics of Jesus." Interesting as that topic might be, it is both elusive—we probably do not have enough firm information to write anything like a rounded account of either Jesus' moral behavior or his moral teachings—and beside the point. This book is interested in Jesus, to put it baldly, only to the extent and in the ways that he is part of the moral world of the first Christians. Naturally, that role is by no means small.

The second topic that is almost entirely absent is the New Testament teaching on this or that: What did the early Christians teach about abortion? About homosexuality? There are three reasons for avoiding questions of this kind, important and fascinating as they are, in this particular book. First, the temptation is too great to subject the early Christians to our agenda. Second, there are many books that deal with such questions; to take them up here would be superfluous and would deflect attention from questions that are not so common: not what the early Christians taught, but how, and, further, what was the symbolic and social universe within which that teaching made sense? Third, compilation of the moral teachings of the first Christians not only oversimplifies the meaning of those teachings by abstracting them from the social reality within which they functioned, it also encourages Christians today to use the Bible in a way that is often pernicious. I hope this book will contribute to the avoidance of Christian nostalgia, which is often confused with Christian faithfulness. Obviously I believe that we have much to learn from the first Christians. And we who are Christians today want in special ways to identify with them and even to submit to their faith and the authority that is theirs by virtue of their standing at the pivotal moment in the Christian story. Nevertheless, they did not have all the answers, and faithfulness is not the same thing as trying to imitate the answers they did have.

What, then, does a historical exploration of the beginning Christian movement's moral formation teach us about how we can be moral people today? Can or should we make the ethos and ethics of the first Christians our own? That is the third topic for which there is simply no room in a book of this size. I expect, however, that those readers who actively engage in the conversation which follows will have their own ideas about how to pursue these other topics.

1

The Social Setting

The town of Athens, in the fifth and fourth centuries B.C., to an astonishing degree created the categories that Western thinkers would use to talk about ethics from that time until our own. One cannot read Aristotle's *Nicomachean Ethics,* for example, without being struck by his reliance upon the common opinion of virtuous men of his own time and place and on the experience of like souls of earlier times, as codified by common sense and folk wisdom. Aristotle's arguments are frequently ad hominem: they persuade not so much by logical demonstration as by appeal to common experience, where "common" means "common to property-owning Athenian citizens." Although Aristotle considered several kinds of constitution and engaged in a great project of collecting and comparing them, his ethic presupposes a settled community whose citizen body was small enough that individuals might interact freely within established social roles. For Aristotle, ten persons obviously do not make a city, but with a citizenry of 100,000 "it is . . . no longer a *polis*" (*Nic. Eth.* 9.10.3). Aristotle is thinking only of the franchised citizens; the total number of residents in the polis might be five or six times as many. Even so, it is worth keeping in mind that by the time Christianity began there were several cities larger than Aristotle's upper limit. But size was only one of the reasons why in first-century Rome, Antioch, or Alexandria it was no longer possible to lead the kind of life that Aristotle was thinking of when he defined the human being as a *zōon politikon*—the kind of animal fit by nature to live in a *polis.*

The Polis as Context of Greek Ethics

The polis, which we translate sometimes "city," sometimes "state," sometimes by the bastard term "city-state"—all three likely to mislead—was a unique invention of the Greeks. Short-lived as a political reality, it retains vitality as an ideal even today. Considerations of size alone, as we have already seen, make it clear that a polis was not quite what we mean by "city." Some *poleis* (the plural of *polis*) each had only a thousand or so citizens; a "village" might be larger. The difference lay in institutions, usually accompanied by physical monuments and arrangements, and in the perceptions and attitudes of the citizens. To be a polis entailed having a formally enrolled citizen body, the *dēmos* (limited ordinarily to property-owning, free males), and a town council *(boulē).* In the ideal case, Athens during its golden age of democracy, the citizens voted in a town meeting or assembly *(ekklēsia:* the word the Christians would adopt, in a rather astonishing act of self-confidence, for their little meetings, which we usually translate "church"), on issues presented by the council. Life in the city was life under laws *(nomoi),* and disputes were settled by argument and, in Athens, by vote of juries before magistrates. The art of persuasive talk was therefore one of the most highly developed skills cultivated by Athenians and Romans. The autonomy and self-sufficiency of the city, its *autarkeia,* was at the center of the pride that its citizens felt, and it included especially the freedom of the polis to settle its quarrels within its own walls. It was, of course, precisely that autarkeia which so soon after Aristotle's time would have to yield to the imperial will of Philip, Alexander and his successors, and then the Romans—who added an alien law and a bureaucracy as well.[1]

Even in its golden age, however, the polis was not free from discord. For Aristotle the good of the polis was identical with the good of humankind, and the science that sought to determine that goal was the master craft above all others *(Nic. Eth.* 1.2.4–8). Most of the proper forms of human association, from that of husband and wife to that of government and citizens, fit neatly together within the polis's structure, like an elegant set of Chinese boxes. The rules for them all could be teased out by closely analyzing the ways of friendship. Yet there is something almost perversely optimistic about this picture. It assumes, for one thing, that all those who occupy the subordinate roles, who therefore participate in the direction of the polis's life only indirectly through their obedience and support of their betters, would be perfectly content so to do. The subordinates included the majority of the inhabitants: women, slaves, and resident aliens *(metoikoi)*.

Furthermore, even before the Hellenistic and Roman empires imposed on the cities a larger dimension of power and authority, there were sanctions and loyalties that for some citizens transcended the polis's laws and could conflict with them. Sophocles' heroine Antigone defies the decree of Creon her uncle, ruler of Thebes, because she thinks it cannot overturn "the gods' unwritten and unfailing laws" *(Antigone* 455), which require her to bury her brother. The struggle is not merely an individual's will against tyranny, but, as commentators since Hegel have observed, the laws of the clan against the laws of the polis. "The girl was expert in her insolence when she broke bounds beyond established law," says Creon (480f.). But for her *his* laws are not the laws of Zeus (450). And if it seems to us most remarkable and exhilarating that it is a woman who stands against the tyrant and the law, Creon knows how to set that fact, too, against the rules by which the polis must be ordered:

> But he who crosses law, or forces it,
> or hopes to bring the rulers under him,
> shall never have a word of praise from me.
> . . . .
> There is no greater wrong than disobedience.
> This ruins cities, this tears down our homes,
> this breaks the battle-front in panic-rout.
> . . . .
> So I must guard the men who yield to order,
> not let myself be beaten by a woman.
>
> (663–677)

The family is in order, according to this view, when it functions as the microcosm of the polis. As men are set over women in the home, so legal rulers are set over their subjects in the city-state. This was the code which, as we have seen, Aristotle would define more prosaically, and which would be repeated centuries after as basic political wisdom. How striking that Sophocles—in whom, along with Pericles, later generations would see the embodiment of the urbane ideal, the Athenian gentleman—would sense and portray so vividly the powerful countercurrents flowing beneath the beautiful surface of the city.[2]

Sophocles was writing at a moment when the power of the independent city-state was at its zenith, more than four centuries before the birth of Christianity. In imperial times, conflicting loyalties threatened the city in yet more complex ways. Sometimes it was foreign cults that, the authorities feared, would undermine public order by teaching wives to disobey their husbands, and slaves their masters, and thus all to cross "bounds beyond established law." The city of Rome on repeated occasions legislated against devotees of the foreign deities Dionysus, then Isis and Sarapis. More than once Jews were ousted, too. To be sure, those measures were exceptional and short-lived; for the most part such cults, including that of the Jews and, after them, that of the Christians, found ways to adapt to the ethos of the imperial city, as we shall see in a later chapter. There were occasions, however, when conflicts between ultimate loyalties could not be avoided. In the Christian martyr-literature of the second and third centuries, there appear several heroines who remind us of less-sophisticated Antigones: the little slave girl Blandina, for example, among the martyrs of Lyons, and the young matron Perpetua with her slave, now sister in Christ, Felicitas in North Africa at the beginning of the third century.

The memoirs of Perpetua—by her own hand, according to the compiler of the whole account—are particularly interesting in their depiction of multiple loyalties that tear at the participants in this nonfiction drama. The civic order is that of Rome, more complex than that represented by Creon. It is not in her hometown Thuburbo that Perpetua must stand trial, but in the provincial capital Carthage, before the *proconsul Africae,* who demands that she sacrifice "for the welfare of the emperors." Family loyalties, too, are more ambivalent. Only when Perpetua's anxiety about the safety of her infant son has been satisfied does she gain strength for her ordeal; after that, when her father brings the child with him to plead with her, she is unmoved. The father, too, represents divided loyalty. As a proper ancient father, he at first demands his daughter's obedience—to him and to the state—for the family's honor. Yet later his mood changes from anger to anxiety and love for her: "With tears in his eyes he called her not 'Daughter' but 'Lady' " (5.5). His persistence annoys the governor, who has him beaten. Perpetua pities him and feels "as if I myself had been beaten" (6.5). Yet she persists, for she has found a new family, in which not only her natural brother but also her former slave are siblings, and she goes to martyrdom "as the beloved of God, as a wife of Christ" (18.2).[3]

These are not stories of everyday life; Antigone and Perpetua were not persons one would meet on every street. Even as dramatic and exceptional characters, however, they exemplify some of the moral crosscurrents that pulled at the inhabitants of the ancient towns in which early Christianity had its main development. In Sophocles' drama, written more than four centuries before the events with which we are concerned, we sense the power of the conflict between the old agrarian family code and the regulation of life in the new and proud polis. In the charismatic martyr story from North African Christians, at the end of the period we are studying, we see that old tension still unrelieved, breaking out anew to disturb the seven-centuries-old identification of noble families' honor with their city's honor. And we see both family code and city code crossed by the claims of new loyalties: an empire on the one hand, on the other a new cult that uses at once the language of city, family, and empire and challenges all three. We must turn back now to survey quickly some of the great changes that had swept across the polis between Sophocles and Perpetua.

The Polis in a World Empire

Rome did not invent imperialism. Athens dominated the other Greek *poleis* in the Delian league, which became the Athenian empire. Resentment of Athens' power, especially in Corinth and Sparta, led to the Peloponnesian War, which left Athens in 404 B.C. defeated, depopulated, and nearly ruined. She rapidly recovered, and Plato and Aristotle taught in a city free and prosperous, in which imperial ambitions were being voiced again. Athens' power, however, would not long endure. The new Macedonian royal dynasty had ambitions on a different scale, more like that of the barbarian empire of the Persians, which Athenians had alternately feared and admired, but resisted. Against Philip, after initial vacillation, Athens was able to hold her own with only minor loss of power and territory, but Alexander overwhelmed her. Alexander's leading generals, after his early death, were soon locked in a struggle with one another, each seeking to wrest control of the vast territory that Alexander had overrun. None could prevail, and by the first decade of the third century the more powerful of them had partitioned the empire. For two centuries more the kingdoms they established would war against one another, in constantly changing alliances with smaller states. Athens sided now with one, now with another, and there were occasionally disastrous results—notably in 262 B.C., when Athens, having been egged on by Egypt in a war against Antigonus Gonatas, was crushed. Like the other old Greek *poleis,* Athens emerged from this period bereft of political power. A last attempt to meddle in world politics, siding with the Pontic king

Mithridates against Rome, brought peremptory punishment from the Romans in 86 B.C. Henceforth Athens would live as a museum of the past. Ambitious young men from good families in the new centers of power would flock to Athens to study philosophy and rhetoric, but the schools themselves had taken their shape in the fourth century and now principally handed on the condensed teachings of the founders and exercised well-tried techniques. The fashions of urban life were set elsewhere, in the huge new cities founded by Alexander's "successors," cities like Antioch in Syria, capital of the Seleucid empire, and Alexandria in Egypt, pride of the Ptolemies. And, of course, Rome, to whom in time all would have to yield.

One result of the transformation of the map of power in the time between Philip and Augustus was that the world perceived by many inhabitants of the lands around the Mediterranean became very much larger. It was mainly the city dwellers whose horizons expanded, but not only they. For example, Italian farmers, for whom in earlier days even a trip to Rome might have been exceptional, might be recruited into, say Sulla's army, to fight in Germany, or in Greece, again in Cilicia on the southern coast of Asia Minor, or even in the wild highlands of Cappadocia, or beyond, following this headstrong patrician into the kingdom of Parthia. For adventurers and romantics, Alexander had become the model, pushing across Persia and even into India. World travels became the ideal not only for conquerors but also for savants gathering the wisdom of exotic peoples—and, on a more prosaic level, a necessity for merchants.

Think, for instance, of the tales of Apollonius of Tyana, journeying to consult with Brahmins in India and Gymnosophists in Upper Egypt. Or witness the monuments of associations of foreign traders who had been drawn to the island of Delos by the first century B.C.: Syrians, Italians, Egyptians, Jews, Samaritans. Consider the tentmakers Aquila and Priscilla, from Pontus on the Black Sea, settled in Rome, then in Corinth, in Ephesus, and finally back in Rome again (Acts 18:2; 1 Cor. 16:19; Rom. 16:3–5). The wise scribe, wrote the Jewish sage Jesus son of Sira early in the second century B.C., "will serve among great men and appear before rulers; he will travel through the lands of foreign nations" (Sirach 39:4, RSV). His grandson in fact moved to Egypt, probably Alexandria, in 132 B.C. and there translated his grandfather's book into Greek. For sage as for merchant, Greek was now the language of the larger world. Knowing Greek, one could, like Priscilla and Aquila, move from Pontus to Rome to Ephesus and do business at once in each place. Yes, even in Rome, for not only was Greek the language of most slaves and freedmen and the immigrant communities in Rome—most Jewish inscriptions of Rome, for example, are in Greek—but also the Roman ruling classes learned Greek with enthusiasm. In part they learned it in order to rule, in the eastern half of their growing empire, but also because of their admiration of Greek culture, beginning already during the Republic. Except in Italy and Sicily, on the other hand, very few Greeks felt impelled to learn Latin.

To know Greek well: to be ready to deliver in public a well-crafted speech decorated with figures Demosthenes might once have used in the assembly of Athens and with snippets from Homer or Euripides—this was the mark of a civilized person. Partly as a result of the dominance and utility of Greek, civilized life meant *city* life even more exclusively than it had in earlier times. In the villages of the eastern provinces, old native languages persisted for centuries, while the cities on which these villages depended now spoke Greek. Another wedge was thus driven between town dwellers and country folk. Village conservatism preserved diversity; urban styles, habits, and values changed in the direction of a single, Greco-Roman culture.

The life of the Greco-Roman city was by no means uniform, however, much less a simple extension of the culture of classical Athens and Sparta or republican Rome. Mixing—syncretism—was the characteristic of the Hellenistic and the Roman eras. The extent of the mixing was especially apparent in Rome itself, and purists hated it. Tacitus, longing at the beginning of the second century for the nobler, simpler values of the Republic, writes that in Rome "all things hideous and shameful from every part of the world meet and become popular" (*Annals* 15.44.3). Here speaks an aristocratic but sensitive writer who recognizes that syncretism produces confusion of moral values. Yet this is only the reverse side of the expansion of possibilities that resulted from the collision of cultures in travel and emigration.

At all levels of society in the cities of the empire we see signs of comparing, assimilating, adding on, testing whether one's ancestral traditions can be put into the language of Plato or Pythagoras. "Doxographies" become popular—something like ancient College Outlines for quick-read students, cataloging the opinions of the leading schools: "The Platonists teach . . . ; the Peripatetics hold . . ." Apologists for "barbarian" traditions could use these to show that their sages were really no different. Josephus tells his Greek readers that of the three Jewish "schools of philosophy," the Pharisees are like the Stoics, the Essenes like the Pythagoreans. The Sadducees, he evidently implies, are like Epicureans (*Antiquities* 15. 371; *Life* 12; *Jewish War* 2.164–165). Much more elaborately and with greater sophistication, Philo of Alexandria undertook to show that all of Plato's wisdom, and the best of Pythagoras and the Stoics, too, were to be found in Moses' writings—allegorically, of course.

Not only the philosophers but the gods of all the lands emigrate, compete, flow together in endless hyphenations of name: Isis the many-named, "among the Thessalians Moon; among the Persians Latina; among the Magi Core, Thapseusis; at Susa Nania; in Syrophoenicia Goddess."[4] At a somewhat more vulgar level, perhaps, the purveyors of magic spells—much in demand, to judge from the number that have survived on papyrus—fill them with real or purported names of deities from every group imaginable, equated to one another or simply added together to assemble more power for the adept.

For anyone in the cities of the Roman empire who reflected on how one ought to act, there were thus loyalties pulling in several directions, and there were multiple teachers, preachers, schools, and spiritual entrepreneurs ready to offer what the Greeks called "guidance of souls" *(psychagōgia)*. The satirist Lucian parodies the competition among the standard schools of philosophy as a slave auction in which different *bioi*—styles of life—are offered to eager bidders. Elsewhere he could as mercilessly lampoon new religious cults and oracles to which adherents flocked from near and far. In this sense the moral world was larger, more diffuse, no longer demarcated by the walls of the polis. To this expansion of horizons there corresponded a growing metaphorical use of "polis" in rhetoric and in some philosophical circles. People attributed to Diogenes, prototype of the Cynics, the saying—when asked where he was from —"I am a citizen of the world *(kosmopolitēs)*" (Diogenes Laertius 6.63). Stoics especially developed this thought in the direction of the universe as one polis, whose king was Zeus or Nature, whose law was the *Logos* or rational structure that pervades and orders reality, and whose citizens were those (very rare!) individuals wise enough to order their lives by that same reason. For the harsher kind of Cynic, however, the kind often seen on street corners in Roman times, the Cynic life meant disdain for the conventions of every city. Utopia was "a city named Begging-bag," as a poem by Crates had put it (Diogenes Laertius 6.85). At the other extreme, apologists for the empire could virtually identify the cosmopolis with Rome, "this polis of the whole inhabited world" (Aelius Aristides, *Orations* 26, "On Rome," 61).

If the citizen now inhabited a larger and more complex world, it did not follow that he had power over more of that world. In many respects the opposite was true. The scope of the individual's political power was obviously much diminished in comparison with the heyday of democratic Athens. No latter-day descendants of Demosthenes and Isocrates would contend in the assembly of Athens or even in Antioch, which would now be the staging area, over the wisdom of the city's raising troops against an eastern empire: that kind of decision would be made in Rome. The pride in being a citizen of a polis was as great as ever; the institutions were still intact. Yet the autonomy of the polis—that meant, even more than before, the autonomy of the minority who were eligible for citizenship and especially of the local wealthy class who were eligible to sit on the city council—was sharply circumscribed. The well-known correspondence between the emperor Trajan and Pliny, the high commissioner he had sent to govern the province of Pontus and Bithynia at the beginning of the second century, is filled with requests from the *poleis* there for permission to do things we would have thought strictly local business. Nicomedia wants a volunteer fire department: No, says Trajan. Prusa would like to replace the old baths: All right, says Trajan, if they can afford it. There is a dispute at Nicaea whether the design of a new theater is safe; Claudiopolis is getting in over its head in building an extravagant new bath; one of Pliny's friends would like to be a citizen of Alexandria—all these matters are carefully referred to the emperor. Around the same time, the famous orator Dio of Prusa was telling the citizens of Tarsus that they had better put an end to the open conflict between their upper classes and the poor linenweavers, else the Roman military delegate would step in, and "I fear that you may lose the right of free speech altogether" (*Orations* 34.39).[5]

From the time that Rome began in the second century B.C. to supplant Alexander's successors, the Hellenistic kingdoms, the map of power had become quite different. As a result, the scope of effective moral decision became different, and more and more dependent upon the place one occupied on the imperial chart. One might still deliver discourses on the character of the ideal king, as Dio of Prusa did on several occasions, expressing traditional sentiments and drawing his illustrations largely from Homer. Yet the speaker must now be constantly aware that the only living candidate for comparison with those ideals was the Roman *princeps*, whom the Greeks had never hesitated to call candidly "king." It was not the Dio wandering in exile, banished by Domitian, who thus spoke of kingship, but Dio restored to imperial favor and speaking, probably, at the court of Trajan (Dio Chrysostom, *Orations* 1–4). The best constitution for a polis was a topic on which philosophers still discoursed occasionally—Plutarch, for example, could take up again

Aristotle's question whether monarchy, democracy, or oligarchy was preferable (*Moralia* 826A–827D)—but the discussion suffered from a certain artificiality.

The Jewish writer Philo could describe Moses as the great legislator of the Jews, more deserving of honor as the founder of an ideal polis than Solon or Lycurgus in Greek tradition (Philo, *Life of Moses* 2.12–20). Yet among Philo's several purposes in writing was propaganda on behalf of his own Jewish community, which occupied a very ambiguous status in Alexandria. That community did in fact enjoy a certain degree of home rule, with its own organization and its own laws, but it was able to do so only by the consent of the Roman prefect of Egypt and in an uneasy balance between native Egyptians, on one side, and full citizens of the Greek polis of Alexandria on the other. The polis for which Moses had legislated was thus, in Roman eyes, only a *politeuma*—an organization of resident aliens—in Alexandria as in other cities of the empire. In time of trouble, the Jews could defend their relative autonomy only by appealing to the Roman emperor. How precarious their situation could be was dramatized when Philo led a delegation to Rome to complain of a pogrom in A.D. 38. The emperor was the egomaniac Gaius Caligula, whose bizarre behavior dismayed the delegation—especially when they learned that Gaius had ordered a statue of himself erected in the Temple in Jerusalem.[6]

Small wonder that in his more allegorical writings Philo undertook to describe a realm where Moses' laws were eternally valid, not subject to the whims of pagan prefects or emperors. That was the city of the wise person's soul, which, ruled by reason rather than by passions, would progress to harmony with the laws of nature itself and, beyond that, to a vision of ultimate Being. In thus psychologizing the concept of the utopian state and thereby narrowing the scope of primary moral concern to those inner choices which lay entirely within the control of the individual mind and will, Philo followed a path well worn by his pagan contemporaries. The path had been opened by Plato, who in his own utopia, *The Republic,* articulated "the idea that justice is man's harmonious agreement with the law within his own soul."[7] It is surely no accident that *The Republic* was one of the most widely read of Plato's works in the Roman period, while his more pragmatic *Laws* was scarcely known. In chapter 2 we shall consider further what is usually called the growing individualism of late Hellenistic ethics, as well as what seems superficially its opposite, the "cosmopolitanism" of some of the philosophical schools. Here, however, we must turn back to the changes in the external world.

Mixed Loyalties: Reactions to Rome

The overwhelming fact on the moral landscape of the first century of our era was the consolidation of Roman power throughout the lands around the Mediterranean. Reactions to that power from Rome's subjects range from intense resentment to effusive praise. From the time of Rome's first major expeditions into Greek territory, prophecies of Rome's eventual downfall began to circulate in the East. Typical of these was a story told of the aftermath of Rome's defeat of the Seleucid king at Thermopylae, in 191 B.C. After the battle Roman soldiers were looting the corpses of their enemies when one of the slain Syrians arose, entered the Roman camp, and there announced that Zeus was angry with the Romans for their desecration of the dead. In revenge he would send a fierce people to Italy to take away the Romans' sovereignty. The Romans sent a delegation to Delphi, only to receive a similar message from the oracle there. Alarmed, they offered sacrifice at the common Greek sanctuary at Naupaktos, but as they did one of their own leaders fell into a trance and prophesied an Asian invasion of Rome, with terrible destruction as its consequence.[8]

Only a few years later, the first clearly datable Jewish apocalypse was written, also predicting the future destruction of a foreign oppressor. The enemy in the book of Daniel, however, was not Rome, but the Syrian kingdom of Antiochus IV, son of the king defeated by the Romans at Thermopylae. While Daniel does not mention Rome, some of the contemporaries of the prophetic author looked to Rome for help against the Syrians. The leaders of the Judeans' successful rebellion against Antiochus, the "Maccabees," also called Hasmoneans, in fact concluded an alliance with the Romans (1 Maccabees 8:17–32; 12:1–4; 15:15–24). Such an alliance suited the Romans' convenience, so long as they were content to balance the Syrians against the Egyptians and to contain the ambition of both. The tiny independent priest-kingdom established by the successors of the Hasmonean rebels could thus count on Roman support for a time. Once Rome moved to take possession of Syria, however, Judean independence could not long endure. A quarrel over succession to the throne and high priesthood between two Hasmonean brothers, Hyrcanus and Aristobulus, brought Pompey into Jerusalem in 63 B.C. Not only the partisans of Hyrcanus, who had won Pompey's support by bargaining and bribery, welcomed Pompey's intervention, but doubtless also many ordinary citizens of Jerusalem, weary of the Hasmonean house's greed and strife, may have regarded him as a liberator. Once it became apparent that Judea would be henceforth a protectorate and tributary of Rome—for a time under Hyrcanus, then under the Idumean Herod as a client king, eventually under direct Roman rule through a prefect or a governor—the ambivalence felt by Judeans became sharper. An anonymous Jewish poet, writing probably not long after Pompey's expedition, remembered it as a judgment of God against the Hasmoneans:

> When the sinner waxed proud, with a battering-ram he cast
> down fortified walls,
> And thou didst not restrain (him).
> Alien nations ascended Thine altar,
> They trampled (it) proudly with their sandals;
> Because the sons of Jerusalem had defiled the holy things of the Lord,
> Had profaned with iniquities the offerings of God.
> *Psalms of Solomon* 2.1–3[9]

But the same poet, or another in the same collection, prayed for deliverance from the new foreign rule:

> Behold, O Lord, and raise up unto them their king, the son of David,
> ·
> And gird him with strength, that he may shatter unrighteous rulers,
> And that he may purge Jerusalem from nations that trample (her)
> down to destruction.
> *Psalms of Solomon* 17.23–24

Similar sentiments were expressed by the rigorist sect that, disgusted by the Hasmoneans, had settled in a desert monastery near the Dead Sea. They applied to the Romans biblical prophecies against the Assyrian and Babylonian empires and wrote a manual of arms for the final "War of the Sons of Light and the Sons of Darkness," for "from ancient times Thou hast fore[told the hour] when the might of Thy hand (would be raised) against the Kittim [= Romans]. . . . For Thou wilt deliver into the hands of the poor [i.e., the sect] the enemies from all the lands, to humble the mighty of the peoples by the hand of those bent to the dust."[10]

Apocalyptic prophecies tend to state moral extremes, but such statements, which could be multiplied many times from the literature of the period, illustrate the deep moral ambiguity that people of the East—and many Italians, for that matter—felt toward the Roman power. That power was awesome and frequently applied in ruthless ways. In the first century B.C. Rome's own civil wars had been fought to a large extent on the soil of eastern countries, bringing new chaos to lands already wracked by struggles among the Hellenistic kingdoms and rebellious local kingdoms. Rome's taxes were experienced as exploitative. Yet, beginning with Augustus, Roman force and civic administration introduced an era of stability and peace that, despite occasional and local disturbances, lasted more than a century. The public spokesmen for moral issues—rhetoricians and philosophers and others of the educated elite—dwelt on the resulting ambiguities no less than did the prophets of conquered groups. They vacillated between describing the injustice of Rome's exploitative power and lauding Rome as the founder and defender of a new order of justice.

Anyone who took the polis to be the primary context of moral authority was bound to be troubled by the overarching power of Rome, which, as noted above, circumscribed local autonomy in a multitude of ways. Similarly, a people with a long tradition of sacral law and custom, like the Jews, would find a thousand irritants in the day-to-day encounters with the Roman provincial administrators. The result might be a militant or subversive opposition to Rome—although revolts were in fact rather rare—or it might be a profound skepticism about the possibility of a just political order. The Romans received a taste of the latter from one of the earliest spokesmen in the city for Greek philosophy, Carneades, the head of the (Platonic) Academy in Athens. In 156/55 B.C., Carneades came to Rome with two other leading philosophers to exhibit there the teachings of the main philosophical schools. Carneades gave two public lectures on successive days. The first argued brilliantly for an ideal of universal justice; the second refuted all his former arguments, showing that there is no justice by nature. Rule, he argued, is by power alone; what makes nations, especially the Romans, great is robbery of others.

The two positions that Carneades set against one another had a long history in Greek thought, going back to debates between the Socratics and the Sophists. The idealist side had already been pressed into service by the defenders of Rome's conquests, and Carneades spoke in part to refute such apologists. We have already encountered the notion that in the polis, as in the household, equity and good order are obtained when those who are fit by nature to rule do so, and those who are by nature suited to be ruled submit. If Rome were thought of as a universal polis, then the very efficiency of her rule could be taken as evidence of her worthiness to rule, and her empire destined by a divine commission to bring nations closer to the "one law, eternal and immutable," as Panaetius put it.[11]

This idealization of Roman government was still being celebrated by some of Rome's provincial subjects three centuries after Carneades' refutation, as Aelius Aristides' famous Roman Oration shows. On the one hand, Aristides said, Rome had fostered the life of the polis: "Now all the Greek cities rise up under your leadership. . . . The coasts and interiors have been filled with cities, some newly founded, others increased under and by you."[12] On the other hand, the quality of justice obtainable now was far superior to that of any autonomous city *(dēmokratia),* because local decisions could now be appealed to a higher court, even to the emperor *(Orations* 26.38–39). There were many provincials who would have agreed with Aristides. We have already noticed the appeal of the Alexandrian Jews to the emperor Gaius. Josephus records several instances of appeals from Jews of the province Asia against local attempts to restrict their freedom.[13] The Roman proconsul in Asia in 62 B.C., Flaccus, was tried in Rome, three years later, for malfeasance, and one of the charges was that he had confiscated Jewish funds collected for the Temple tax.[14] And in Acts 25:10–12 we see Paul exercising his rights as a Roman citizen to appeal to Caesar against an accusation by his fellow Jews in Jerusalem.

In at least one respect, however, Aristides' encomium of Rome's justice deserves skepticism. He claimed not only an evenhanded administration of justice in all parts of the empire but also for people of all social levels: "There is an abundant and beautiful equality of the humble with the great and of the obscure with the illustrious, and, above all, of the poor man with the rich and of the commoner with the noble."[15] This claim is particularly ironic because—beginning already in the time of Hadrian and continuing in the reign of Antoninus Pius, the emperor whom Aristides praises so effusively in this speech—the law codes made a formal distinction between treatment proper to "the more honorable," that is, the upper classes, and "the more humble," everybody else. The stratified society was a constant fact in the world of antiquity, and, as Aristides recognized by his idealization, must be taken into account in any discussion of ancient ethics.

The Stratified Society

Society in the high Roman empire was much more closely and rigidly divided than the societies most of us are used to. People tended to identify themselves and others by their social locations, and these locations on the social grid deeply affected their expectations for themselves and others' expectations of them. Tombstone inscriptions routinely boasted not only of family but of all offices held and important deeds performed, for those of higher status. Even those of lower rank would boast of what they could, identifying themselves, for example, by the initials *s.* for *servus* or *serva,* "slave," or *l.* for *libertus* or *liberta,* "freedman" or "freedwoman." How much weight the social categories carried depended to some extent on the place one lived, whether Rome or the provinces, whether large town or small, and certainly whether polis or village, town or country. Thus there was no unified social system for the whole empire, but a series of ranking systems that, viewed from the top down, over-lapped, while for humble folk only one might be directly relevant.

One way of visualizing the whole is by thinking of the following, greatly simplified, groupings.[16] At the top is a collection of people who carry out the leading functions in the empire as a whole; their power and prestige derive from ad hoc arrangements that emerged with the empire. There was no legal entity corresponding to what we call "empire," any more than there was, legally, an "emperor": Augustus had nodded to Republican sentiment by calling himself simply *princeps,* "the First" (of the Roman citizens). Nevertheless, the actual power of the princeps was unmistakable—the Greeks regularly called him "king"—and so was that of the people whom he advanced to govern the sprawling lands that the Romans had acquired. These included the members of the princeps' household and of his council, those senators and knights who were made pre-fects or governors of provinces, and some distinguished jurists. The second grouping was the traditional Roman aristocracy: senators and knights, their privileges determined by descent, by wealth, and by formal induction into their respective "order." The anomalies of the imperial situation were dramatized not only by the emperor's increasing ability to make or break both senators and knights, but by the fact, galling to traditionalists, that in the first century an emperor's freedman who held one of the important offices in the new bureaucracy was more powerful than most senators. Third, there was in every provincial city a local aristocracy as well, on the local scene as grand to those beneath them as were the senators and knights of Rome, although their light grew pale whenever there was occasion to compare it with the Romans, and although their actual autonomy was limited in many ways, as we saw earlier, by the pres-ence of the provincial government. With these local nobles of the city-councillor class might be ranked certain intellectuals who had gained renown as orators or philosophers.

The three categories listed so far comprised probably less than one percent of the population of the whole empire. It is sobering to recognize that these are the ones we know best, for they produced most of the surviving literature, and their picture of the world is taken for granted by most histories of antiquity even now. It is very hard to classify the rest, the vast majority, but it is important to recognize that they did tend to classify themselves and one another. Even slaves within a household ranked themselves; those with more desirable jobs had higher prestige than menials and had the fact recorded on their tombstones: "nurse," "pedagogue," "valet." Some of the indices of higher status were these: Roman citizenship, especially in the provinces in the early years of the empire, when it was rare; citizenship in the local polis, compared with resident aliens; among the citizens, the decurions or city councillors of smaller cities; wealth, more and more, preferably inherited rather than worked for, and invested in land rather than trade; family and origin: the older the better, the closer to Rome the better, Greek better than "barbarian"; military office or the status of veteran in a colony; freedom by birth, though a freedman or even a slave of the emperor or of a senator was better off than many freeborn persons.

Most people living in one of the cities of the Roman empire, then, were constantly aware of rank on rank of others above them in the social pyramid, and the distance from top to bottom was very great. There was, moreover, little or no expectation that the ranks would change. No organizations existed that were dedicated to social change, and we hear of only rare and local rebellions by oppressed groups. There were no revolutionary movements in antiquity. Nevertheless, it is clear from the description above that the development of empire had imposed some new structures on the traditional rankings, and that meant that there were new possibilities for movement up or down the scale and for the mixing of categories. The case of imperial freedmen or slaves outranking some of the hereditary nobility in sheer influence has already been mentioned. Naturally the way others judged such parvenus depended on the observers' place in the hierarchy; satirists fond of the old aristocratic values regularly lampooned people who had inherited money but lacked good taste and manners, or aristocrats who had sunk to indulge in vulgar pursuits like acting or gladiatorial show. Most ordinary people could expect to remain on the social level of their parents. Still, they did in some numbers consult fortune-tellers who could tell them whether a dream might mean the chance of a big inheritance that would change their lives, or something dreadful, like having to enslave oneself because of unpaid debt; or who could cast the horoscope of their son, which might portend a happier future, perhaps through the act of some wealthy patron. Rising on the social ladder was rare, but it did happen; sinking happened, too. When one did rise, from slave to free, from decurion to knight to senator, the change depended on the goodwill of someone higher up in the social scheme. That had much to do with the stability of the system.[17]

The close stratification of the society profoundly affected the moral perceptions and moral choices of its members. The scope of an individual's power to affect events varied enormously with one's place in the scheme, and therefore the kind of moral issues about which one would be likely to think seriously varied widely, too. What we would regard as the really big decisions—war and peace, coping with natural disasters and other emergencies, the empire-wide administration of justice—became more and more, over time, the province of the emperor, his advisers, and his agents. Some of those philosophers and orators who were, or wanted to be, the king's advisers developed what we might call a supply-side theory of morality. That is, corresponding to the steep pyramid of social power, they conceived a kind of ethical pyramid with the king, under God, at its peak. The king, as a kind of living law, ought to embody the rational harmony and order of nature itself, so that his decrees and specific laws would reflect that order, and all his subjects, benefiting by the justice the king decreed and learning to imitate his soul's harmony thus made visible, might enjoy that same universal harmony.

From the bottom of the pyramid, things looked a lot messier, no doubt, yet there was a very widespread perception that, if justice were to be possible, it would have to come from someone higher up who had power. The appeals recorded on numerous scraps of papyrus preserved in Egypt make vivid this hope on the most mundane level:

> To Apion *strategus* from Sambous daughter of Amois. . . . Certain matters are the subject of legal proceedings between me and Apion son of Demetrius, and Dionysius son of Dionysius, his mother being Demetria, from the same city. They have assumed forcible possession of property belonging to my cousin Demetrius also called Diogenes, it being of the value of 10 talents, and a part of it being mine by title of inheritance. . . . In addition I have a dispute against one of the parties, Apion, over a debt of 1 talent he owes my deceased mother Arsinoe. . . . All these matters require the judicial decision of the excellent prefect Vibius Maximus. I therefore request [all these parties to be summoned to the next meeting of the district court].

In crises, the appeal might be to someone even higher up: "Lusianias inquires of Zeus Naios and Dione whether the baby Annyla is carrying is really his." Or on a larger scale, "Behold, O Lord, and raise up unto them *their* king. . . ."[18]

Social location is also a factor in ancient definitions of both duty and equity. One ought to do what was "fitting," and that meant fitting for one of your status and role. Even in the period of the high Roman empire, when philosophical ethics focused more and more on the autonomous decisions of the individual, the contexts within which those decisions were exercised were still the traditional roles. For example, the famous speech with which the Roman Stoic Epictetus responded to a young man who considered becoming a Cynic —the most individualistic of ancient philosophical movements— begins by warning that everyone's true role in life is determined by God. For, just as every well-run house has a master, "so it is also in this great city," the world. Here too there is a house master who assigns each his task:

> "*You* are a calf; when a lion appears, do what is expected of you; otherwise you will smart for it. *You* are a bull; come on and fight, for this is expected of you, it befits you, and you are able to do it. *You* are able to lead the host against Ilium; be Agamemnon. *You* are able to fight a duel with Hector; be Achilles." But if Thersites came along and claimed command, either he would not have got it, or if he had, he would have disgraced himself in the presence of a multitude of witnesses.[19]

We are not concerned here, as we shall be in the following chapter, with Epictetus' Stoic attempt to define the wise person's inner freedom, which transcended all external constraints. The point here is that, in spite of that ultimate aim of his philosophy, he defines vocation and duty in terms of conventional roles.

Aristotle had already spoken in some detail on this question, for example, within his discussion of friendship, a category for him that encompassed many aspects of social and political life. What is "proper and fitting" depends on relationships, he observes. Thus the honor that is owed differs from one category to another: father, mother, a great philosopher or general, an older person, colleagues and brothers, kindred, fellow tribesmen, fellow citizens, and the rest (*Nic. Eth.* 9.2.7–10). In book 5 of the same work, Aristotle had introduced a similar principle into his discussion of justice. Justice entails equity, but equity is not the same as numerical equality. It is rather fair proportion, "since the ratio between the shares will be equal to the ratio between the persons; *for if the persons are not equal, they will not have equal shares*" (5.3.6).[20] This was true of the distributive justice necessary for good order in a polis, but in a slightly different way also for "corrective" justice, which Aristotle applied to private transactions. Without fair proportions being established between goods and services and—above all—honor exchanged, "there will be no exchange and no community [*koinōnia*]" (5.5.10).

Despite occasional utopian statements in the literature, like Aristides' claim, quoted above, that rich and poor received the same justice, the pervasive sentiment in antiquity was that what people deserved depended on where they stood in the social order. Perhaps what Aristides meant by "equal" was "proportional" in Aristotle's sense. As we saw, it was actually legislated in Aristides' time that "more honorable" people would receive lesser punishments for the same crimes than "the more humble." That had been the practice long before it was published in writing. One of the things Philo complained about in his account of the misdeeds of the prefect of Egypt in A.D. 38 was that when the latter arrested Jewish elders he flogged them with whips ordinarily used for the lowest classes of the city, the Egyptian-speaking noncitizens, rather than the flat paddles used for Alexandrian citizens, a privilege previously accorded also to the Jewish residents (*Flaccus* 78–80). Paul demands an apology from the Philippian officials who have beaten him and Silas, not because they were falsely charged, but because this was done *publicly* to *Roman citizens* (Acts 16:37). The first readers of Acts would have understood that what was at stake was an affront to the *honor* due to anyone of that relatively high status. As Paul advised the Roman Christians, echoing a commonplace, "Remit to everyone what is owed: tribute to the one (deserving) tribute; taxes to the one (deserving) taxes; fear to the one (deserving) fear; honor to the one (deserving) honor" (Rom. 13:7, my trans.). When he begins the next section, "Owe no one anything but to love one another" (13:8), we sense that some alternate set of values has suddenly intruded. Yet the smoothness of the transition, carried by Paul's reprise of the word "owe," shows that he sees here no sharp discontinuity between the two.

The exchange of goods, services, and prestige, in proportion to the socially assigned "worth" of each participant, was the process that, Aristotle suggested, made ancient society work. (Certain modern sociologists have argued that every society can be analyzed on the same principles.) Honor and shame were the reciprocal sentiments that enforced the unwritten rules of these continual transactions. It is enough for Epictetus to say, in his hypothetical example of a man seizing a role for which he was unsuited, that Thersites would have put himself to shame before "a multitude of witnesses." For a citizen to be treated as an alien was to be put to shame. For a slave or freedman to put on airs like a freeborn citizen marked him as shameless. For an emperor to give performances like an actor or musician, as Nero is said to have done, was a public shame. You must do, as Epictetus said, "what is proper to yourself"—and that meant, proper to the role in the universe that nature has assigned to you.

Thus, in the society within which Christianity came to birth, one's ordinary sense of what was fair, what was expected, what was honorable depended upon one's place in the social pyramid. Consider, as a final example, this saying attributed to Jesus in the Gospel of Luke:

> Which of you whose slave has been plowing or herding the sheep, when he comes in from the field will say to him, "Come right away and sit down at the table"? Will he not rather say to him, "Fix my dinner and get yourself ready to serve it to me until I have eaten and drunk; afterwards you also may eat and drink"? And he will not thank the slave for having done what he was ordered to do, will he? In the same way *you* ought to say, when you have done everything that was commanded you, "We are useless slaves; we have done (only) what we were obliged to do." (Luke 17:7–10, my trans.)

Outside the City

So far we have been talking about life in the Greek and Roman cities, because that was the social context that shaped the major visible traditions of ancient ethics, and the context in which the expansionist form of early Christianity took shape as well. As the passage just cited from the Gospel reminds us, however, the beginnings of the Christian movement were in the rural and village culture of Palestine. In later centuries—later than the period this book deals with—when Christianity from the cities would penetrate into the countryside, differences between the culture of the city and the culture of the village would pose very large problems for the church. We must therefore notice here that those differences existed; we shall return briefly to them in chapter 4.

The great changes wrought in the Mediterranean map by the Hellenistic kingdoms and the rise of the Roman principate did not alter the fundamental dependence of the ancient economies upon agriculture. However exuberant the life of the new and old cities, it would have been impossible without the farms of the surrounding, supporting countryside, called the *chōra* in Greek. On the other side, the villages were dependent on the cities in a multitude of ways. Yet between them, more often than not, hostility festered: urbane people looked down their noses at the rustics, thought them crude and backward, and did not scruple, often, at taking advantage of their simplicity. Peasants viewed the city folk with suspicion or fear.

Things were not helped by the steady tendency for more and more land to be owned by fewer people, and those comfortably living in the cities or in their suburban villas.

From the beginning of cities, there had been conflict between the values of family and clan and the values of the city-state. We have seen how that conflict was dramatically registered, in the golden age of Athens, by Sophocles' *Antigone*. In every generation, in some measure, the conflict was repeated in the life of everyone who migrated from village to polis. The old values and sanctions of clan and *ethnos* (the larger "national" or "racial" community; neither term in its modern usage is appropriate to the ancient scene) endured longer, unself-consciously, in the village than in the city. Differences in language between city and *chōra* in many parts of the empire, differences in the scale of social encounter, differences in the speed of change, all helped to insulate the old ways.

Nevertheless, there was a steady seepage of values from polis to village, following the gradient of power and prestige. To be civilized was to be city-like; what ambitious person would not want to be thought civilized? Rural tombstones are rarer than those found around cities, naturally, but wherever they are found, they echo the style of the urban epitaphs, with however many misspellings, and praise similar virtues of the deceased. We must also reckon with some flow of values in the opposite direction, for there was a continual migration of people from country to city, and agrarian romanticism in certain urban writers never completely died out.

2

The Great Traditions: Greece and Rome

Ancient writers who described their society generally looked at it from the top down. We shall have to do that, too, initially: "the great traditions" are those that were cultivated by the educated elite. There is a certain irony in calling these "great," for, as the anthropologist Robert Redfield pointed out, the "predominant form of human living throughout the history of mankind" has been what he calls "the little community."[1] Small, homogeneous, self-sufficient and self-contained, it is in many ways the opposite of the expanding, pluralist network of Greek and Latin cities in the Roman empire, where the "great" traditions were at home. Unfortunately, to learn very much about life in the little communities of the ancient past is tantalizingly difficult. We will be able to correct the elite perspective imposed on us by most of the extant sources only in fragmentary ways. For example, we will consider traditions of some who were alienated from the urban culture within which they lived (like the Cynics) or who formed alternative communities (like the Epicureans and some Jews). The Christian writings themselves will give us a glimpse of a broader cross section of society than appears in the high-culture literature. We begin, however, with the more visible and explicit statements of the society's values.

The great traditions are those which are borne by a literary canon. For the subject of this chapter, that canon comprises the philosophical heritage of classical Greece, the rhetoric of Greece and Rome, and the epic and dramatic literature to which both constantly referred. In chapter 3, the scriptures of Israel will be at the center of attention. In both cases, we should not be misled by calling the core of the tradition "literary." It was not by reading books so much as by *hearing* them recited, listening to public speeches, attending lectures, hearing sermons and homilies and exhortations that one learned the tradition. That is why rhetoric is as important for our purpose as philosophy.

Philosophy in the Roman Empire

Beginning in the late Republic, the Romans adapted Greek philosophy; they did not invent their own. Cicero, for example, translated and paraphrased large chunks of Greek philosophy and acquainted his readers with the tenets of the leading schools. Musonius Rufus, who has been called "the Roman Socrates," lectured in Greek, and a century later the philosophical emperor Marcus Aurelius wrote his *Meditations* also in Greek. The schools that had taken form in classical Athens continued—or were in some cases perhaps reborn—to have some sense of identity. Seneca, for example, who *did* write in Latin, could contrast "our" (Stoic) beliefs with those of the Epicureans and others (*Epistles* 9.20; 33.1f.; etc.). Lucian, in his *Lives for Sale,* parodied the peculiarities of the major schools, as they were popularly perceived or misperceived. A literary convention developed in which the writer spoke of having tried each of the schools in turn before having discovered the true philosophy; the Christian apologist Justin Martyr introduced himself this way (*Dialogue with Trypho* 2). Nevertheless, it is debatable how distinctive the different schools really were in Roman times. Certainly they influenced each other considerably. It is also hard to be sure to what extent the schools were organized entities; in most cases it seems likely that a "school" was only a lecturer and his pupils who met in whatever place they found convenient.

In Roman times, the principal schools of philosophy were more and more concerned about ethics, or perhaps we should say, the moral formation of the soul. Philosophers and sophists still gave lectures "on kingship" and "on the constitution of the city" and the like. Yet in the age of empire, as we saw in the previous chapter, most of their attention had come to focus on the republic over which the wise person still had some control: his own soul. An anonymous tract, *The Education of Children,* which has come down to us among the works of Plutarch, tells us that the study of philosophy ought to cap a proper education. Why? Because "for the soul's maladies and passions the only medicine is philosophy."[2] The tract then outlines what the pupil should learn from philosophy:

> What is honourable and what is shameful, what is just and what is unjust, what, in brief, is to be chosen and what to be avoided, how a man must bear himself in his relations with the gods, with his parents,

with his elders, with the laws, with strangers, with those in authority,
with friends, with women, with children, with servants; that one ought
to reverence the gods, to honour one's parents, to respect one's elders, to be obedient to the laws, to yield to those in authority, to love
one's friends, to be chaste with women, to be affectionate with children, and not to be overbearing with slaves; and, most important of
all, not to be overjoyful at success or overmuch distressed at misfor-
tune, not to be dissolute in pleasures, nor impulsive and brutish in
temper.[3]

This outline suggests a rather static picture of the way the world
works and especially of the way society is organized. The different
schools of philosophy had different notions of what was ultimately
real about that picture and somewhat different ideas about the way
the educated person should act toward that reality. All agreed,
however, that each person's task was the shaping of the self.

In our necessarily very brief look at each of the "Great Traditions," it will therefore be useful to concentrate on the profile of the
moral biography that each school sketches out, subordinating to
those sketches two other large questions. What is the world of
meaning within which the virtuous person lives out his or her life?
What is the character of the good person? How are the two connected?

A summary of "Platonism," "Stoicism," and so on in the few
pages available here would be vacuous. Instead we will look at a
representative of each—remembering that representatives worth
talking about do not merely represent. They also think for themselves and sometimes contradict not only received opinions of their
schools but even things they themselves have said elsewhere.

The Platonists: Plutarch

L. Mestrius Plutarchus was a young man when most of the New
Testament books were being written; he died sometime after A.D.
120. He lived most of his life in the small town where he was born,
in the central section of Greece called Boeotia, but he had wide
connections. He was a rhetorician and biographer, but he also regarded himself as a professional philosopher of the school of Plato,
and historians of philosophy today treat him as the primary representative of Middle Platonism at the beginning of the second century.[4] Plutarch was also a deeply religious person. He was a priest
at Delphi for the last thirty years of his life and often refers to that
shrine and to its principal god, Apollo, in his philosophical writings.

He also did research on other cults: on Isis and Osiris, for example, and on ancient Greek and Roman religious practices.

In a dialogue that Plutarch composed on a detail of the Delphic shrine (like Plato he favored the dialogue genre), the final speaker observes that everyone who approaches Apollo at Delphi receives the greeting, "Know yourself," to which the proper reply is, "You are." This exchange suggests, says Plutarch's spokesman, that God alone *is,* and to know oneself aright is to acknowledge that "we possess no share in genuine being," for we are caught in ceaseless change, becoming and passing away, like a succession of countless births and deaths. Being is eternal, unified, unchanging. Human life is temporal, multiple, constantly changing.[5] Here Plutarch succinctly announces the metaphysical tension of Plato's world and the human task of Platonic ethics. The good life is one that leads from our common plight of multiplicity and change to "genuine being."

The goal toward which every successful life aims, for Plutarch and the other Platonists, is to be like God.

> Consider first that God, as Plato says, offers himself to all as a pattern of every excellence, thus rendering human virtue, which is in some sort an assimilation to himself, accessible to all who can "follow God." (*On the Delays of the Divine Vengeance* 5 = *Moralia* 550D)[6]

How does one accomplish the task of becoming like God? The Delphic oracle tells the starting place: knowing oneself. The key is knowledge, and both the means and the enabling ground are reason, for reason is the human faculty that makes saving knowledge possible and also that power which we share with the divine.

Plutarch, like other Platonists, has great confidence in education. Virtue is teachable; how can it not be?

> Men learn to play the harp, to dance and to read, to farm and to ride the horse; they learn to put on shoes and to don garments, they are taught to pour wine and to bake meat. All these things it is impossible to do properly without instruction; but shall that for the attainment of which all these things are done, that is, the Good Life, be unteachable, irrational, requiring no skill, and fortuitous? (*Can Virtue Be Taught?* 1 = *Moralia* 439B)[7]

However, learning virtue is more difficult than learning to ride a horse. The knowledge that is required is not merely acquaintance with facts and propositions, but a transformation that involves the will. The road toward divine likeness can be taken only by someone who turns deliberately away from the flickering shadows on the wall of the cave, in Plato's famous parable, to face the light, the Idea of the Good, which is the source of all true being. Plato had used for this "turning around" of the "whole soul" a group of words for which Cicero would use the Latin *conversio* (*On the Nature of the Gods* 1.77), and which Christian writers would take up later to denote "conversion" to the Christian faith.[8]

The "conversion" to a philosophical life, moreover, is only the beginning of a struggle, a contest whose prize is virtue and happiness. The primary opponents in this contest are aspects of oneself, for the soul itself is divided. One part is godlike, "true and attracted to excellence and rational"; the other part is "irrational and attracted to falsehood and emotional" (*How to Tell a Flatterer from a Friend* 20 = *Moralia* 61D–F). The former pulls the self in the direction of unity and order and indeed of God, but the latter tends toward disorder. The individual soul shares this composite nature with "the soul of the universe," of which it is "a portion or copy" (*On Moral Virtue* = *Moralia* 441D–F), and there are passages where Plutarch can speak of a rather ominous dualism of the universe itself, based on a remark in Plato's *Laws*. The world is moved, he says, not by one soul but by at least two, the one beneficent, "the other the opposite and making opposing things" (*On Isis and Osiris* = *Moralia* 370F). The rational part of the human self and of the universe is thus up against an irrational element that is not merely the absence of reason, but opposed to it. Here is a dark side of the Middle Platonic picture of reality that would proliferate in the Gnostic systems of the second century and beyond, while later Neoplatonists would reject it. This dual picture of the world and the soul distinguishes Plutarch's view, by his own account, from the monistic picture of the Stoics.

The Stoics and Plutarch agree that virtue is achieved by reason conquering the emotions. They disagree on the question whether the emotions are a real, independent part of the human self, and whether they have any positive role in the moral life. Plutarch spells out the disagreements in his essay *On Moral Virtue* (*Moralia* 440D–452D). In the first two chapters he surveys the views of a number of Stoic philosophers, which he then summarizes: "All of these men agree in supposing virtue to be a certain disposition of the governing portion of the soul and a faculty [or "potential," *dynamis*] engendered by reason, or rather to be itself reason which is in accord with virtue" (*Moralia* 441C). The emotions for these people, he says, are not a separate, irrational part of the soul, but only reason gone astray: "a vicious and intemperate reason" (441C–D). The truly wise person for the Stoic is one whose decisions are unaffected by emotion; the ideal state of mind is *apatheia,* "impassivity." (Stoics contemporary with Plutarch had in fact moderated this classic position, but Plutarch presents the older, extreme case for the sake of contrast.)

Against the Stoic view, Plutarch insists that "moral virtue," as opposed to "contemplative," purely intellectual *(theōrētikē)* virtue, "has as its material the emotions *(pathos)* of the soul and as its form reason *(logos)*" (440D).[9] The work of reason is not to cut out emotion altogether, but only to prune it and cultivate it, for emotion remains "a necessary part of [a person's] being" (451C). What has to be learned is to follow the mean between extremes, as Aristotle had taught. A wise man does not hamstring spirited horses and oxen, but tames them; when reason tames the emotions, they are even more useful than horses and oxen. "Anger, if it be moderate, will assist courage, and hatred of evil will aid justice, and righteous indignation will oppose those who are prosperous beyond their deserts" (451E, Helmbold).

The well-lived life is thus for Plutarch a Pilgrim's Progress from foolishness to wisdom, from vice to virtue. Plutarch objects vigorously to the old Stoic doctrine (which, again, few Stoics of his own time would affirm in this form) that divided all humankind into only two categories, the very few wise and the very many foolish.

> But as for us, we observe that there are degrees in every kind of evil, and especially in the indeterminate and undefined kind that has to do with the soul. (In the same way there are different degrees of progress produced by the abatement of baseness like a receding shadow, as reason gradually illuminates and purifies the soul.) (*How a Man May Become Aware of His Progress in Virtue* = Moralia 76B)[10]

Moral progress requires constant practice *(askēsis),* for there is no standing still in philosophy (76D). Habit *(ethos)* is a valuable helper to reason in shaping moral character *(ēthos,* ibid.), for it trains both the body and the irrational element of the soul, as domestic animals are trained, so that "even if their driver lets go the reins," they stay in the right paths (82F–83E).

The Stoics: Musonius Rufus

Caius Musonius Rufus was born around the time that Jesus died, and he lived until the end of the first century. He was a key figure in the vigorous revival of Stoic philosophy that occurred under the Roman principate and in the connection of that philosophy with public affairs. He was no ordinary teacher, but a Roman knight who took into his intimate circle young men of high promise. Most of them, probably, were also ambitious children of Roman aristocrats, but they included the slave Epictetus. Musonius argued that women, too, should study philosophy, but there is no record of any women among his own pupils. The persons who studied with him include the two figures of the next generation in philosophy and rhetoric who are best known to us, Epictetus and Dio Chrysostom, and others equally famous in antiquity, like Artemidorus, who married Musonius' daughter. Among those in later generations who were deeply influenced by his teachings were the Stoic Hierocles and the Christian Clement of Alexandria.

Many of the stories about Musonius that circulated in ancient times had to do not with his philosophy but with his conflicts with imperial authority. He was involved in the opposition to Nero, and when Nero punished the conspiracy against him led by Piso in A.D. 65, he banished Musonius to the barren island of Gyara. Recalled by Galba after Nero's assassination, Musonius was banished again by Vespasian. The tension between such engagement with the political order and the ideal of the philosopher's autonomy with respect to all "external things" is one of the most intriguing aspects of Musonius' teachings.

In contrast to the prolific Plutarch, Musonius wrote nothing that has survived. What we have of his teachings are only a few anecdotes and sayings, remembered by Epictetus and others, and notes of dialogues he held with his pupils, which were compiled into essays, it seems, by one of them. Twenty-one of the latter were gathered into ancient anthologies, along with some fragments from other sources; these have been brought together in modern editions.[11] These remains do not give us a complete picture of what went on in a Stoic school. The technical language in which Stoicism abounded, the exercises in logic for which it was famous (see Lucian, *Lives for Sale* 20–25), and systematic discussion of basic doctrine are all lacking. Nevertheless the corpus is particularly useful for our topic, for all the questions Musonius deals with in these remains are ethical ones. Indeed, Musonius taught that it is with ethics that philosophy is finally concerned. Philosophy, he said, consists in "thinking out what is man's duty and meditating upon it" (No. 16; Lutz, p. 107). And it was as an ethical system that Stoicism from Musonius' time forward had its most enduring influence.

Everyone wants to be happy. All the major schools of Hellenistic-Roman philosophy accept this premise and affirm that happiness (Greek *eudaimonia*) is the perfectly proper goal of a well-lived life.

They present philosophy as a kind of therapy which will guide a serious student to that end. Being happy, however, is not the same thing as feeling happy: more often the opposite. Like the Platonist, the Stoic insists that in order to achieve real happiness we must learn to distinguish it from transient pleasures, which only *appear* to be related to happiness. He agrees, too, that learning this distinction is a matter of repeated, deliberate choice, a lifelong struggle for rational mastery.

To be happy, in this enduring sense, is to be like God. Musonius can describe the human being as "the only earthly copy" or "image *(mimēma)* of God" (No. 17; Lutz, p. 108, 8f., my trans.). When a person is virtuous, then, he is like God and therefore "happy." This sounds like Plutarch's Platonist version of the chief end of man, but on closer examination it turns out to be different. More fully, the passage reads:

> In general, of all creatures on earth man alone resembles God and has the same virtues that He has, since we can imagine nothing even in the gods better than prudence, justice, courage, and temperance. Therefore, as God, through the possession of these virtues, is unconquered by pleasure or greed; is superior to desire, envy, and jealousy; is high-minded, beneficent, and kindly (for such is our conception of God), so also man in the image of Him, when living *in accord with nature,* should be thought of as being like Him, and being like Him, being enviable, and being enviable, he would forthwith be happy, for we envy none but the happy. (No. 17; Lutz, p. 109, italics added)

The key concept here is "nature," and that is what Stoics generally mean when they say "God," although Musonius and his pupil Epictetus sometimes use such personal expressions when talking about God or Zeus that we may wonder whether they did not hold a kind of piety that was not altogether consistent with their Stoic pantheism. Be that as it may, they agree that to live a good life one must live "in accord with nature."

If we imagine that maxim to mean the same as "doing what comes naturally," we will completely miss the point. When we say "behaving naturally," we usually mean following our emotions or our drives, and that is very nearly the exact opposite of what the Stoics mean by following nature. Nature for the Stoics has a rather austere and abstract face; what counts is the "right reason" *(orthos logos)*, which gives to nature its form and meaning. We might translate "the rational structure" of the universe. Sometimes the Roman Stoics speak of it as "the *law* of nature." Now the human self is a "copy of God" because the self's "ruling part" is itself *logos,* reason. Hence we have the capacity to live in harmony with the rational structure of the universe, and such harmony is our rightful destiny.

Virtue is therefore natural. "All of us, [Musonius] used to say, are so fashioned by nature that we can live our lives free from error and nobly" (No. 2; Lutz, p. 37). "For the nature of each [creature] guides it to its own excellence" (No. 17; Lutz, p. 109). If that is the case, however, it is hard to see why wisdom and virtue are so exceedingly rare, as the Stoics think they are—especially since, unlike Plutarch, they recognize no maleficent principle at work in either the individual soul or the soul of the world. The root of evil seems to be only ignorance and false opinion, and that can be overcome by careful thought and training.

Obviously the question, How is it that I can act unnaturally? borders closely on the larger issue in Stoic ethics, How can freedom of any sort exist in a universe that has rational law built into its very matter? What survives of Musonius' dialogues tells us, unfortunately, almost nothing about what he said on this issue. However, it was a topic that Stoics and their opponents debated endlessly in antiquity, and modern students of Stoicism have found it no less perplexing. Opponents objected that, if the world were as strictly determined as Stoics seemed to think, it made no sense to praise or blame people for acting rightly or wrongly; that is, there was no basis for moral evaluation. Musonius, like the other Stoics, quite obviously does urge people to make moral choices, and that entails, as he often says, that one can choose badly. Yet, when one chooses rightly, one is choosing what is one's destiny; when one chooses wrongly, one chooses futility, for then one is foolishly trying to cut against the very grain of the universe. One of the fathers of Stoicism (the metaphor is attributed to both Zeno and Chrysippus) put this graphically by comparing the human situation with that of a dog tied behind a cart. Either the dog can run freely along with the cart, or he can be dragged. The dog has a real choice, and which choice he makes effects a material difference in his life: happiness or misery. Further, if he understands his situation he will surely choose to go with the cart and be happy. "Of the things that exist," said Musonius, "God has put some in our control, others not in our control." The intelligent person begins by understanding which is which and acting accordingly. "We ought in every way to lay claim to the things that are in our control, but what is not in our control we ought to entrust to the universe and gladly yield to it whether it asks for our children, our country, our body, or anything whatsoever."[12]

Since our responses, our uses of such internal reactions, are the only thing we can control, not the external world itself, *moral* choice has to do only with the former. That alone is the realm within which things count as good or bad, which means simply, virtues or vices. Only virtues are truly good; only vices are truly evil. Exile, for example, which Musonius experienced more than once, "is not an evil." Only false opinion makes it seem so. If one says that exile deprives one of freedom of speech *(parrēsia)*, Musonius replies, "Fear is the cause of this, not exile." Virtues cannot be taken away by exile: "Certainly the exile is not prevented from possessing courage and justice simply because he is banished, nor self-control, nor understanding, nor any of the other virtues. . . . But if you are bad, it is the evil that harms you and not exile; and the misery you feel in exile is the product of evil, not of exile" (No. 9; Lutz, p. 75). Virtue alone is both necessary and sufficient for happiness. And virtue is entirely within a person's own control.

All "external things," that is, everything but the choices we make about the mental impressions which alone we control, are morally "indifferent" *(adiaphora)*. By Musonius' time the Stoics had softened their absolute and equal disregard for all externals. They now recognized that, while they still insisted that externals could not be either good or bad in the strict sense, nevertheless some were "preferable" while others ought to be "rejected." In between were others that were strictly neutral, truly "indifferent."

If the wise person does not allow himself to care strongly about anything not under his control, the result is a kind of asceticism. Musonius' pupil recorded several fragmentary discourses on food, clothing and shelter, and furnishings, as samples of things Musonius used "frequently" to talk about (Lutz, Nos. 18A–B, pp. 19, 20). These portray an austere life. The overarching virtue is self-control *(sōphrosynē,* verb *sōphronein)*, which is exhibited in choosing food that is cheap and natural to humans—vegetables, grains, milk, and cheese, for slaughter is natural to beasts of prey, not civilized beings —and comparable simplicity in the other necessities. The sage should regard clothing, for example, as a soldier thinks of armor: the best is what provides protection, not what attracts attention. The influence of the Cynic movement, strong in Stoicism from the beginning, is visible here. The Roman Stoics admired the Cynics, or at least some Cynics whom they regarded as the authentic ones, and two of Musonius' pupils have given us vivid pictures of the ideal Cynic as well as of his counterfeits (Epictetus, *Discourses* 3.22; Dio Chrysostom, *Orations* 32.9–11). Musonius and his pupils were not as severe in their asceticism as many of the Cynics, but they agreed with them that the test of philosophy is learning to disdain hardships (see Musonius, No. 7; Lutz, pp. 56–59).

Nevertheless, the Stoic does not *choose* hardships, even though he welcomes those that come, as "showing the man" (Epictetus, *Discourses* 1.24). Furthermore, there is no such metaphysical dualism behind the Stoic asceticism as there was in some forms of Middle Platonism. For the Stoic, mind and body are both material, and the mind or soul of the individual will not, any more than the body, survive the dissolution that comes at death. That dissolution, too, is a natural event and therefore cannot be evil. When the great rhetorician Isocrates called death "the last of evils" (compare Paul's "last enemy," 1 Cor. 15:26), says Musonius, he showed he was no philosopher, for "how could there have been any smattering of knowledge of or acquaintance with true good and evil in the man who thought that an evil which is the necessary sequel even to the best life?" (No. 17; Lutz, p. 111).

The doctrine of the sage's "self-sufficiency" *(autarkeia),* his disdain for all "externals," makes the Stoic sound like a radical individualist. Early Stoics, like Cynics always, underlined the isolation of the sage by dividing all humankind into only two classes: wise persons and fools. There was no middle ground. Chrysippus had remarked that you drown just as surely a few inches beneath the surface as at the bottom of the pond (Plutarch, *Against the Stoics on Common Conceptions = Moralia* 1063A). So, no matter how near one came to moral perfection, one was not yet a sage until one's virtue was complete. Nevertheless, Chrysippus spoke also of the life of progress toward this perfection. In later Stoics idealization of the sage goes so far that Seneca remarked that, like the phoenix, a good man appears only once every five hundred years (*Epistles* 42.1). If perfection is so rare, the philosopher's concern must practically be with those people in between, who are making progress toward wisdom and goodness. Hence for Musonius as for Plutarch, the career of the person who chooses virtue is the story of a contest, a struggle to win rational control, which alone produces ultimately virtue, wisdom, and therefore happiness. The *prokoptōn* or *proficiens,* the person still engaged in that struggle, is not yet immune to the external restraints that affect all humans, nor superior to the duties imposed on all members of society.

Responsibility for the public order is, accordingly, a prominent theme in Musonius Rufus' discourses, as it is in the writings of his students. Of all animals, it is the bee that is most like the human, for "it bends its energies to the one common task of his fellows and toils and works together with his neighbors" (No. 14; Lutz, p. 93). Marriage, the basis for social life, is taught by nature. "For, to what other purpose did the creator of mankind first divide our human race into two sexes, male and female, then implant in each a strong desire for association and union with the other? [Musonius is tacitly alluding to Aristophanes' creation myth in Plato's *Symposium*]. . . . Is it not then plain that he wished the two to be united and live together, and by their joint efforts to devise a way of life in common?" Everyone should think of his own household as a wall around the city, and the beginning of that wall is marriage (ibid.). Even the Stoic's description of the ideal Cynic defines that radically autonomous figure as God's gift to the society. He does not live for himself, but for all humankind, whom he has taken as his children (Epictetus, *Discourses* 3.22.23, 46, 81f.).

Like other philosophers of his time, Musonius seems to have taken for granted that monarchy is the natural form of government, arguing only that the king ought to study philosophy, "if, indeed, he is to be a 'living law' as he seemed to the ancients" (No. 8; Lutz, p. 65). This acceptance of monarchy did not, of course, oblige the philosopher to obey royal commands that did not seem to him in accord with "the law of nature." Musonius himself was at least sympathetic to the conspiracy against Nero, whether or not he was involved in the actual plot.

The person progressing toward wisdom thus lives within the social structures of obligation, yet in case of conflict his only ultimate obligation is to the transcendent norm which is variously called reason, nature, or God. One must obey one's father—so long as one understands that *real* obedience means to follow nature. If the parent, being no doctor, orders something harmful to health, or, being wicked, orders something immoral, then to do what he says is really disobedience, and to refuse is really obedience (No. 16; Lutz, p. 107).

There is a tension here between the philosopher as social being and the philosopher as autonomous judge of good and evil. Viewed from one angle, the Stoic ethic is self-referencing. "I continue to maintain," says Musonius, "that everyone who sins and does wrong, even if it affects none of the people about him, yet immediately reveals himself as a worse and a less honorable person" (No. 12; Lutz, p. 87). Yet "honor" and its opposite, "shame," are ordinarily norms created by a society. Musonius recognizes this, but wants to redefine them:

> Men who do not know what is really good and what is shameful, having regard only for common opinion, think they are insulted if someone

gives them a malignant glance or laughs or strikes them or reviles them. But the wise and sensible man, such as the philosopher ought to be, is not disturbed by any of these things. He does not think that disgrace lies in enduring them, but rather in doing them. (No. 10; Lutz, pp. 77–79)

The philosopher's action in such cases has nothing to do with altruism. The wise person will not go to court against anyone, choosing to ignore or to forgive wrongs done him, not out of care for the offender, but for the sake of his own independence. Ironically, Musonius' own argument for this position—at least as his Boswell has paraphrased it—after all has an eye to public opinion, to the way the philosopher "appears" (*phainesthai*). As Lutz translates, "How much better a figure does the philosopher make so conducting himself as to deem worthy of forgiveness anyone who wrongs him, than to behave as if ready to defend himself with legal procedure and indictments, while in reality he is behaving in an unseemly manner and acting quite contrary to his own teaching" (ibid., 79–81).

The Stoic who is still progressing toward true wisdom cannot flout the ordinary rules of social behavior with that "shamelessness" celebrated in so many anecdotes about Diogenes, the prototypical Cynic (see below). Those rules, which specify what is "appropriate" (*ta kathēkonta* or *officia,* often misleadingly translated "duties") in the conditions of life in which he finds himself, have a positive role to play in guiding him along his way. Nevertheless, they belong only to the intermediate range of "preferred" but ultimately "indifferent" values.[13] The Stoic wants finally to be autonomous, independent of all such values, to be immune to what others count as honor and shame as well as to any coercion, and that means of course to be independent of the society itself.

The Cynics

The Cynic embodied that quest for autonomy to which the Stoic reasoned. That is why we find Cynics idealized in works of Stoics in the Roman period. Indeed it is only with some irony that we can place the Cynics among the "great traditions," for the Cynics—especially those figures most sharply drawn in the anecdotes and apothegms that survive—prided themselves on being outsiders. Moreover, we hear rather often of the Cynic preacher appearing in public, always identifiable by his rough cloak, long, unkempt hair and beard, staff, and begging pouch, haranguing passers-by or people gathered in the market. That kind of Cynic (sometimes mentioned with disdain by philosophers and satirists) seems closer to the world of the masses than to the literary elite. Nevertheless, the Cynic movement traced its roots to Antisthenes, contemporary of Socrates, and sometimes claimed Socrates for its own. And there was a Cynic literary tradition. The following sketch is based on a collection of pseudonymous letters, attributed to such worthies as Socrates and Antisthenes and their disciples, which are thought to have been written at various times from the third century B.C. to the third century A.D.[14]

The Cynics are a different case from those philosophical schools considered so far. Were they in fact a *school* in any strict sense, either as offering organized instruction or as possessing a system of doctrines? This was debated in antiquity, with some insisting that Cynicism was not a "philosophy" but only a "way of life" (Diogenes Laertius 6.103). It seems fair to speak of a loose movement, rather than school, of individual teachers (from their style one is tempted rather to say "prophets"), who do not so much argue for a coherent world view as provide models and provocation for a consistent and radical way of living. Cynics were impatient with philosophical talk. Yet the Cynic Epistles do reveal a high level of interest in the intellectual problems we have seen discussed by the Platonists and Stoics. The Epistles themselves represent a will to argue rationally for the Cynic life, and therefore a more philosophical Cynicism than is perhaps represented in many of the popular stories told about Diogenes and others or by the wandering, begging preachers.

We are told several times that Diogenes discovered the "short cut to happiness" (Crates 13; Malherbe, p. 65; 16, p. 67). "For the way that leads to happiness through words is long, but that which leads through daily deeds is a shortened regimen" (Crates 21; Malherbe, p. 71). "Diogenes" expands the metaphor in one of the fictional letters addressed to his father, in which he reports his own conversion by Socrates. Socrates had pointed out two roads, one which went straight up the side of the Acropolis, "the other long, smooth, and easy." The two roads to happiness, he said, were like those. Diogenes immediately chose "the steep and rough road," as he said, "since I was superior to the hardships" (Diogenes 30; Malherbe, p. 131).

Here we encounter again a notion which we met in both Plutarch and Musonius, that a happy life can only be achieved by struggle and effort. Those philosophers agree with the Cynics, too, that "happiness is not pleasure" (Crates 3; Malherbe, p. 55). Like the Stoics, the Cynics identify happiness with virtue, and "virtue is something acquired by practice and does not spontaneously enter the soul as evil does" (Crates 12; Malherbe, p. 62).

What does the Cynic practice? The simple life. "Practice being in need of only a few things (for this is the closest thing to God)" (Crates 11; Malherbe, p. 63). The way to contentment is not by trying to get all one desires, but by learning to desire little.

> Accustom yourselves to wash with cold water, to drink only water, to eat nothing that has not been earned by toil, to wear a cloak, and to make it a habit to sleep on the ground. Then the baths will never be closed to you, the vineyards and flocks fail, the fish shops and couch shops go broke, as they will to those who have learned how to wash with hot water, to drink wine, to eat without having toiled, to wear purple clothing, and to rest on a couch. (Crates 18; Malherbe, p. 69)

To renounce possessions is the beginning of wisdom. It was said of Crates that he deeded all of his property to his home city of Thebes and, standing in the public assembly, announced, "Crates, son of Crates, sets Crates free" (Diogenes 9; Malherbe, p. 103).

Freedom was a watchword of the Cynics, and that meant self-sufficiency *(autarkeia)*. Freedom from possessions was only the starting point and outward sign of a deeper freedom, however: freedom from false opinion. The emblems of the Cynic—the heavy, rough cloak worn summer and winter and serving as a blanket by night, the staff, the knapsack—set him or her apart from everyone living according to ordinary conventions. To live in accord with nature is what is needed—again the Cynics agree with the Stoics—but nature "has been banished from life by appearance" (or "conventional opinion," *doxa:* Diogenes 6; Malherbe, p. 97).

To escape from conventional opinion is difficult; a cure of seeing only appearances requires drastic medicine. That is why we often hear conversion stories in the Cynic traditions, and why the conversions are so often provoked by a Cynic doing something that shocks all ordinary sensibilities. Diogenes persuades a free-for-all boxing *(pancratium)* champion that his victory is foolishness (Diogenes 31; Malherbe, pp. 132–137). He spits in the lap of a very wealthy young man who invited him to dinner, the room being so grandly decorated there was no place else to spit (Diogenes 38; Malherbe, p. 163). Both give up their former lives and take the Cynic emblems.

The "shamelessness" with which the Cynics attacked convention was celebrated in stories and pithy sayings, especially of Diogenes.[15] In a society in which honor and shame were the most constant sanctions for guarding acceptable behavior, some of the actions attributed to Diogenes were so outrageous that Cynicism might seem determined to undermine the whole social order. Not only does "Diogenes" open his lunch during someone else's lecture, or anywhere else when he feels hungry, he also masturbates in public and, rebuked, says he only wishes he could relieve hunger as readily by rubbing his stomach. Such behavior led to many witty puns, by friend and foe alike, on the nickname "Cynic," taken by its opponents to mean "doglike." The Cynic shows no respect for authority; Diogenes, meeting Alexander the Great, asks only that the king get out of his light.[16]

Nevertheless, Diogenes belongs to the city; his exploits require an audience and aim for a response. Although his way of life seems to be a radical individualism, yet the Cynic does not become a hermit. In the Roman period there was a debate within the Cynic movement itself about the relationship a Cynic ought to have with the people around him.[17] Some Cynics hold the public and all the normal functions of society in utter disdain. They abandon all ties to the usual institutions and wander from place to place as beggars. They confront and insult people, not because they expect to gain converts, but in order to demonstrate their own superiority to the masses. A Cynic, they say, is not made but born. Other Cynics, however, are known for their gentleness and patience, accommodating their rigorous message to the capacity of their audiences. They are like physicians who may have to prescribe harsh medicines, but who have the welfare of their patients at heart.

In neither case do the Cynics work for the transformation of the social order. The austere type of Cynic implicitly gives up on finding any good within settled society. The mild Cynic takes the common institutions of polis and empire for granted and justifies his own disengagement from them by the benefit he would render if people would heed him. Either way, the focus is entirely upon the individual's actions, either in utter disregard of the social institutions or within them.

The mission of the Cynics is, by provocative words and actions, to challenge people to think about their lives and purposes. Those who are able to hear awaken from thoughtless acceptance of conventions and appearances and instead focus their efforts on the few things that are real. The Cynic, however, does not offer any intellectual program for deciding what is real. The arguments in the Cynic Epistles are philosophically eclectic and often ad hominem. The Cynic conversion stories do not depict people who think carefully through metaphysical issues and arrive at conclusions, but people who are jolted out of their routines by some provocation that exposes those routines as silly. The challenge to free oneself from popular opinion implies accessibility to a transcendent norm, but the Cynics do not tell us what such a norm might be. The shortcut is to act, not talk.

The Epicureans

The Epicureans, too, were self-conscious outsiders and were treated as such. By the time Christianity was coming to be known, almost everyone stereotyped the Epicureans as antisocial lovers of pleasure, and detractors of the new Christian cult sometimes compared it with them. Stoics like Epictetus regularly denounced them, and Plutarch wrote a tract against them, archly entitled, "That It Is Not Possible to Live Pleasantly in Epicurus' Way." Often it seemed that only such acid observers of society as the satirist Lucian could find the Epicurean view of the world congenial (see, for example, his *Alexander the False Prophet*). Nevertheless, some Roman intellectuals of the late Republic had admired aspects of Epicurus' teaching. One of them, Lucretius, became an enthusiastic Epicurean and wrote the elegant didactic poem that is our major surviving source for Epicurus' physics. Even under the empire, the Stoic Seneca quotes often from Epicurus. Conversions to the Epicurean way of life, for which there is good evidence from an earlier period, probably continued.

As in the case of the Cynics, we can most readily gain a picture of the Epicureans by looking at a sample of their internal literature current in the first two centuries of our era. Epicurus, who was born just seven years after Plato died, wrote a huge quantity and organized his school to study his own works systematically. Well into late antiquity there were groups still reverently studying them, but most of the books have been lost. Apart from some fragments found on papyri at Herculaneum and some quotations by ancient authors, what we now have are three letters, two of which are probably authentic and are concise summaries of Epicurus' physical and moral teachings respectively, and a collection of maxims called "Basic Doctrines"—these four all preserved by Diogenes Laertius in the tenth book of his "Lives"—and another collection of maxims found in a manuscript of the Vatican library and hence referred to as "Vatican Sayings."[18]

"The greatest fruit of self-sufficiency," said Epicurus, "is freedom" (*Vatican Sayings* [hereafter *VS*] 77). That could have been said by Plutarch, Musonius, or any of the Cynics as well, but the way in which the Epicurean pursued self-sufficiency was different from the others. The Epicurean was not a gadfly to the urban crowds, but withdrew from public life altogether to live in quiet seclusion with other Epicureans. The model of their life was the garden of Epicurus' house in Athens, where the original group used to meet; the school was therefore called "the Garden" *(kēpos)*. There it was possible to lead the "private life" that Epicurus advocated (Plutarch, *Moralia* 1128f. = Frag. 86; Bailey, p. 139). The rhetorical commonplace, that it was impossible to please the crowds, was attributed with special appropriateness to Epicurus (Frag. 43; Bailey, p. 131), for he "laid down the dogma that the human is not by nature either a social animal or civilized" (Themistius, *Oration* 26 = Usener, *Epicurea*, No. 551). Indeed, "we must release ourselves from the prison of affairs and politics" *(VS* 58).

The Stoic Epictetus found that idea outrageous, of course, and attacked the inconsistency of Epicurus in making use "of the very principle that he is doing away with" *(Discourses* 2.20.6), since the friendship of Epicureans among one another was famous. If Epicurus had really believed what he said, Epictetus continues, he would not have written "such big books" to keep people from being deceived. Epicureans of the Roman empire did write propagandizing literature. In the second century A.D. one of them, a certain Diogenes, "out of compassion" for his fellow citizens of Oenoanda erected a stone billboard in the marketplace, inscribed with a summary of Epicurus' teachings. Further, Epicureans commissioned statues of Epicurus and other leading figures of the school, which seem to have been designed to exhibit to sympathetic members of the public the ideals of quiet grace, wisdom, and contentment to which they believed Epicurean training led.[19] Nevertheless, they generally heeded Epicurus' admonition not to become engaged in political affairs. The "big books" were circulated among the "friends" who had already been converted to Epicurus' way. And the friendship which they prized was not a product of nature but of wise choice. It is evident, then, that, while the Epicureans, too, could speak of their life as "according to nature," they understood "nature" and their relationship to it quite differently from the Stoics.

"Of all the things which wisdom acquires to produce the blessedness of the complete life, far the greatest is the possession of friendship," said Epicurus *(Basic Doctrines* [hereafter *BD*] 27; quoted also by Cicero, *About the Ends of Goods and Evils* 1.65). But friendship is so important for the sage precisely because he recognizes that by nature individuals are utterly separate from one another, and "each cares only for himself" (Frag. 523, Usener). The first principle of friendship is the discovery of mutual advantage *(VS* 23). That leads to a kind of social contract, which permits society to arise. Yet dependence of any sort runs counter to Epicurus' notion of happiness. One of the reasons he denies that the gods could be concerned with human affairs is that "troubles and anxieties and feelings of anger and partiality do not accord with bliss, but always imply weakness and fear and dependence upon one's neighbors" (Diogenes Laertius 10.77, trans. R. D. Hicks, Loeb Classical Library). Evidently he thinks of real friendship as a freely chosen relationship, a kind of contract, which does not limit freedom. Evidently, too, the Epicureans did not think that such a dialectic between freedom and mutual support was possible in the society of the Greco-Roman city, but only in the small, family-like cells that they formed in private households.

What then did it mean to the Epicureans to live in accord with nature? The Epicureans had a very special conception of the physical universe, and that conception formed the basis for their ethic. Although Epicurus did not think highly of the standard form of education, warning one pupil to "flee from every form of culture *(paideia)*" (Bailey; Frag. 33 = Diogenes Laertius 10.6), he did urge the study of physics, that is, of nature *(physiologia)* (*Epistle to Herodotus* = Diogenes Laertius 10.35–83; Bailey pp. 18–55). The world is composed of atoms, that is, indivisible particles, which would all fall in straight, parallel paths at a uniform rate of speed, except for one thing. In some way which the Epicureans apparently did not explain, a random factor is introduced; the atoms "swerve." This irregularity of their motion makes collisions possible, and the collisions in turn occasionally produce a clustering of atoms into worlds, of which ours is neither the first nor the last.

Everything happens then as a result of utterly mechanical causes, and those, as in modern atomic physics, are infected by a certain indeterminacy. The reason why it is so important to learn this, according to the Epicureans, is that this knowledge dispels illusions. We need neither fear mysterious powers in the universe nor expect too much from nature. The gods have nothing to do with running the universe; if they did it would make them busy and anxious, and anxiety is incompatible with happiness and therefore with being gods. We do not, therefore, have to worry about offending the gods, but on the other hand we cannot look to them for help. They care nothing about us. We live in a world of physical atoms and a society of human atoms. *That* is the nature to which we must adjust our lives and in which we must work out our own salvation.

The other way in which the Epicureans differed radically from the other philosophical schools active in Roman times is their unabashed approval of pleasure *(hēdonē)* as a goal of life. The others were careful to distinguish happiness *(eudaimonia)* from pleasure, especially sensual pleasure. Epicurus, however, taught that "No pleasure is a bad thing in itself: but the means which produce some pleasures bring with them disturbances many times greater than the pleasures" *(BD* 8). Aiming for pleasure does, contrary to other philosophies, accord with nature: "We must not violate nature, but obey her; and we shall obey her if we fulfill the necessary desires *[epithymiai,* another pejorative term for most Hellenistic moralists] and also the physical, if they bring no harm to us, but sternly reject the harmful" *(VS* 21). The qualifying clauses in these sayings are, of course, important, but it is easy to see why Epicurean doctrines offended many.

To make matters worse, the Epicureans denied that the good and therefore happy life was difficult. They refused to apply to the well-planned life that favorite metaphor of all sorts of other Hellenistic moral guides, the athletic contest *(agōn).* "He who has learned the limits of life knows that that which removes the pain due to want and makes the whole of life complete is easy to obtain; so that there is no need of actions which involve competition *(agōn)" (BD* 21).

Yet the pleasure with which the Epicureans' life was "filled up" —a phrase they often used—was in fact very austere. They defined pleasure as the absence of pain. "The pleasure in the flesh is not increased, when once the pain due to want is removed, but is only varied" *(BD* 18).

> When, therefore, we maintain that pleasure is the end, we do not mean the pleasures of profligates and those that consist in sensuality, as is supposed by some who are either ignorant or disagree with us or who do not understand, but freedom from pain in the body and from trouble in the mind. For it is not continuous drinkings and revellings, nor the satisfaction of lusts, nor the enjoyment of fish and other luxuries of the wealthy table, which produce a pleasant life, but sober reasoning, searching out the motives for all choice and avoidance, and banishing mere opinions. *(Epistle to Menoeceus* = Diogenes Laertius 10.131f.)

When real physical needs were satisfied, when withdrawal from public affairs removed most threats from outsiders, and when training in the Epicurean world view removed irrational fears of death, then life was complete. "The mind, having attained a reasoned understanding of the ultimate good of the flesh and its limits and having dissipated the fears concerning the time to come, supplies us with the complete life, and we have no further need of infinite time: but neither does the mind shun pleasure, nor, when circumstances begin to bring about the departure from life, does it approach its end as though it fell short in any way of the best life" (*BD* 20).

Some Common Themes

Despite their differences, the major philosophical movements we have sampled all agreed that the aim of philosophy is the well-wrought life. Ethics is the craft of right living, and it has to be learned. The one reliable tool that one has for sculpting the good life is reason. Reason must of course be accompanied by practice, and the various schools understand the relation between reason and practice in different ways. Some of the Cynics despise book learning and present practice as if it were the only important thing, but even they implicitly acknowledge the central role of thought in distinguishing between reality and appearance.

All agree, too, that the rational and therefore happy life is a life in accord with nature, although their conceptions of nature, including human nature, differ. Because what is natural has been obscured by error and by social conventions, all require an austere reasoning process and a strict discipline in order to carry out the maxim, Live in harmony with nature. There is thus a certain asceticism in the philosophical life. The philosophers mistrust emotion. The ideal of the early, orthodox Stoa was a sage who showed no emotion at all; most philosophers of the Roman period aimed at a careful moderation of passion. Even the Epicureans, who unlike the others regarded pleasure as unequivocally good in itself, stressed the limitation of desire as the way to achieve the untroubled life.

Some modern commentators have discerned in philosophies of the Roman age a trend toward egalitarian social thought. If the rankings of people are not by nature but by convention, then they are ultimately of no importance. Thus, while Aristotle thought some persons were destined by nature to be slaves, neither a Plutarch nor a Musonius would agree. The only important distinction is between the wise and the foolish. Musonius had slaves among his pupils and taught that women, too, should study philosophy. Cynics recalled the stories of Hipparchia, a Cynic as stalwart as her husband Crates. The Epicureans, however, seem actually to have practiced the egalitarianism others talked about. The original Garden had included slaves as well as free (though the slaves were not manumitted until Epicurus died), and women, both courtesans and wives. Yet while the hierarchical roles did not have ultimate significance, the philosophers we have looked at were far from wanting to abolish them. Moreover, all shared an implicit intellectual elitism. Only a few persons could be wise and therefore virtuous and happy. What is usually left unsaid is that only a very few could afford the leisure and money to study philosophy.[20]

In one respect all the philosophers of the imperial age are disappointing. It seems to us in retrospect that the fundamental issue of the times must have been how the humane values achieved in the classical polis and the Roman Republic could be made effective in the vastly enlarged and transformed political and social world of the empire. Yet the writers we have looked at address that issue indirectly at best; more often they seem implicitly to acknowledge its enormity by avoiding it. It is common today to speak of the individualism of Hellenistic and Roman philosophy, and there is a certain truth in that, but the term needs to be carefully qualified. The mind of the sage is the measure of all things, yet the sphere of action even for the sage consists to a surprising degree of conventional roles whose naturalness is rarely questioned. Even the revolt of the Cynics against convention hardly goes beneath the surface. It may be particularly enlightening to meditate on the paradox of the Epicureans. They were the ones who most completely surrendered the public affairs of the polis as the arena for exercise of virtue, and who backed their ideal of the autonomous individual by a world view in which what is ultimately real is atoms. Yet they withdrew not to monastic isolation, but to the "garden" of friends. It was as if, mistrusting the new structures of power that operated now behind the still-standing facade of the polis, they turned back to the relationship that all ancient philosophy regarded as the foundation of civil society, friendship, to create in their intimate fellowship a microcosm in which reason and virtue could still survive.

Transmitting Moral Traditions

How were values and moral ideas passed along from one generation to another? Obviously this is a very large question, and an answer to it would involve, as a minimal starting point, analysis of the whole ancient system of education.[21] What is possible here is only the sketchiest of outlines of those institutions and relationships within which the dominant cultural and subcultural values were transmitted.

Education began, of course, in the family. Even though schools had become common by imperial times, the father remained primarily responsible, in ancient sentiment, for educating his dependents, or seeing that they were educated. The language of ancient wisdom literature reflects this: "Hear, O sons, a father's instruction" (Prov. 4:1); "Listen to me your father, O children" (Sirach 3:1). This had become conventional in the speech of the professional sage of the East, but even in republican Rome Cicero addressed his great treatise *On Duty* to his own son. The head of the household had to make sure that not only his children but also his other dependents learned what they needed for their roles in life. There were schools, for example, for slaves, and often slaves were trained for specialized work: stenography, accounting, and other commercial skills, medicine. We know of at least one slave, Epictetus, whose master let him study philosophy with the famous Roman Stoic, Musonius Rufus. Some of the older literature on marriage suggests, too, that the male head of a household was obliged to educate his wife, who married, on average, at an age between twelve and fifteen. What these old manuals had in view was only training her to manage the household properly. By the period with which we are concerned, however, it had become common for boys and girls, from the age of seven, to attend school together, and in many ways, at various levels of society, women were somewhat less subservient. It is impossible to calculate exactly what proportion of the free population may have received a primary schooling. Probably it was not large, even in those towns where the schoolmaster was paid by an endowment or by municipal funds. Literacy in the empire, by very rough estimate, did not exceed 10 percent on average. We would be safe in assuming that most children in poorer families continued to receive only what learning their parents could provide at home; children of artisans would at an early age become apprentices to their own fathers or to other craftsmen. There is some evidence that mothers came to exercise a larger role in the teaching of their children than had been the case in earlier times.[22]

What children learned, at the primary stage of education, was mainly to read and write. In the process, continuing into secondary school with a "grammarian," they committed to memory certain set pieces from Homer, portions of Euripides' tragedies, bits of Menander's comedies, some of the speeches of Demosthenes, and other samples of what had become a classical canon. Mechanical as the learning procedures were, their teachers understood this to be a fundamental part of the moral formation of the children. The heroes of the Iliad were patterns of life for the Greek; no educated person would ever be at a loss to cite a personal example of vice or virtue, drawn from Homer and the other classics.

For those who could afford a higher education, both the schools of rhetoric and the major schools of philosophy concerned themselves in the Hellenistic and Roman periods very largely with ethical questions. Such an advanced education was mostly for an elite, but it had a much broader influence. The students who enrolled in Epictetus' school at Nicopolis were no doubt mostly ambitious young men from aristocratic families of Rome and the provinces, but Epictetus himself had begun his study of philosophy as a slave. His admiration of the Cynics, whom he described as "scouts" of God, shows his concern for the public moral significance of philosophy. Others went further. His contemporary Dio of Prusa, so famous as an orator that subsequent generations called him "the golden-mouthed," *Chrysostomos,* derided people like Epictetus who lectured only in the controlled setting of a classroom, "possibly because they despair of being able to improve the masses." He also despised most of the "so-called Cynics," who, he said, were really panhandlers and, though they did speak to crowds, only led people to mock at philosophy. Dio himself was prepared to speak to a large, public audience in the city's theater (he spoke these words, in fact, in the theater of Alexandria), and precisely for their moral improvement.[23] Listening to speakers, whether the street-corner Cynics or people like the charismatic Apollonius of Tyana (later idealized by his biographer as a Pythagorean philosopher), who might intersperse his admonitions with exorcisms or other miracles, or professional orators who might perform in the theater or a rented hall or the salon of a wealthy patron, was a popular diversion among people of all classes in the ancient city. The speeches not infrequently dealt with moral themes.

Among the indirect ways in which moral questions were kept before ordinary people, we must consider the effects of public legal process. It was in advocacy on one side or the other of legal cases that most of the orators trained in professional schools found their employment, so it was in the courts—generally held in some portico, a public basilica, or the open forum—that anyone with time to listen could readily hear the time-honored moral themes and examples applied to some particular dispute or alleged crime. In spite of the immense efforts made by the Romans at systematizing and codifying the law (although the codes we know best were compiled later than the period we are concerned with), there remained vast areas of legal decision that were not determined by precise precedents, and that must be decided case by case in relation to some general view of what was just and fair. The practice of law, then as now, was to a large extent a matter of moral persuasion. Furthermore, not only Roman law was involved. For local matters, the Roman governors gave room for decision on the basis of Greek or native law, and in specific instances, the best known being that of the Jews in certain cities, a large and well-organized immigrant community might receive the special privilege of deciding cases involving only its own members on the basis of the traditional law of that group's homeland. Thus for Jews of, say, Sardis and Alexandria, the study of biblical laws and their elaboration and interpretation was no merely "religious" obligation, but an integral part of the limited self-government permitted the community. At the same time, because of the ambiguous situation of these Diaspora communities, confrontation between ethnic laws and morals and those of the politically dominant Hellenistic and Roman law and power was always present, at least potentially. This fact not only gave a strong impetus to the study of the tradition, it also affected the way the tradition was understood. Think, for one perhaps rather special example, of Philo. As we noted briefly in the previous chapter and will see at greater length in the next, Philo insisted on maintaining the distinctive practices of Judaism, while expounding the Torah in such a way that Moses was made to teach very nearly the same central virtues that a contemporary pagan philosopher found in Plato or Chrysippus.

There were a number of ways in which the Jews constituted a special case among the ethnic groups with strong traditions, not least in their relatively high level of literacy. Both the power of their traditions and the fact that Judaism was the immediate context for the emergence of the Christian movement now require our particular attention.

3

The Great Traditions: Israel

The matrix from which the great traditions of Israel were born was not the polis. To be sure, in the Hellenistic age Israel had to come to terms with the polis, and her traditions were never the same afterward. When the reformers of Jerusalem in the second century B.C. undertook to establish there a polis, with a gymnasium, a Greek-speaking citizen body, and other institutions and values of a Hellenistic city, the result was a violent confrontation, which we call the Maccabean revolt.[1] The Maccabees defeated the Hellenists, but that did not end matters. Not only did the dynasty of the Maccabees exhibit more and more characteristics of a Hellenistic kingdom as time passed, but also the Greek traditions and institutions continued to exercise enormous power over the imagination and thinking of many in Israel, not only in the Diaspora but even in the homeland. Some Jews tried to show that what Moses had to offer, in the sacred books of Israel, was the greatest polis-constitution of all. Nevertheless, even those Jewish thinkers who strove most prodigiously to assimilate the Greek learning to the books of Moses demonstrated, by the very energy which their enterprise required and by the shape of the results, that they began with quite a different notion of the social structure within which human responsibility is exercised.

What was that different structure? It was a very complex and variable set of institutions, rituals, beliefs, stories, and rules, which we can sum up under the phrase "the people of God." The fundamental context of Jewish ethical reflection was not the polis or the individual, but Israel. And Israel was construed as a people under the special orders and protection of the one God.

Israel's traditions were formed through a long historical process too complex to review here. During the nodal period of their formation, the political context was a tiny, precarious monarchy of a sort found all around the eastern coast of the Mediterranean, under the shadow of the great empires of the Fertile Crescent. Yet during the monarchy Israel preserved specific collections and cycles of older traditions from the time when "there was no king in Israel," but only tribes and confederations. On the other side, most of the definitive work of compiling the traditions into scripture came in post-monarchic times, when Israel was no longer independent but under the hegemony of a succession of more powerful states, from the Persians to the Romans. Each stage left its mark.

The Situation

From the Babylonian exile in the sixth century B.C. until the beginning of the Byzantine empire, roughly a millennium, Jewish life was stamped by a strong polarity between homeland and Diaspora. The Jews were not unique in this respect. This period, and especially the middle centuries of Rome's ascendance, was an age of migration, and immigrants who preserve an ethnic identity always experience tension between their new environment and their former ways. For Israel, however, the tension was peculiarly acute because of the significance of the Land in their sacral traditions and symbols. God's promise of the Land to the patriarchs, a promise fulfilled in the exodus and Joshua's conquest, is an organizing theme of the books of the Torah. Torah and Prophets frequently speak of separation from the Land as punishment (e.g., Deut. 28:36–46; 29:22–28; Jer. 15:13–14). Yet in the Roman era the large majority of all Jews lived outside the Land of Israel. Some, indeed, had been exiled by force, but most had emigrated voluntarily, and many had lived in the Greek cities around the Mediterranean for generations. They rarely thought of themselves as "exiles."

The status of Jews in Greek cities of the eastern Roman provinces and in Rome itself was ambiguous. That was true of any group of aliens resident in a polis, but more so for the Jews because of the strength of the special beliefs, institutions, and symbols that gave them their identity as a people. Circumcision, avoiding work and business every seventh day, refusal of pork and certain other foods, absence from every civic ritual or festival that involved any sacrifice or recognition of any god but their own—all these constantly reminded them and their children that they were a people apart. They also reminded the other groups of the city, who often resented what they saw as the "misanthropy" of the Jews. At the same time, the urban Jews wanted to participate as fully as they could in the life of the city. They proudly called themselves "Alexandrians" or "Antiochenes" or "Sardians," and campaigned for rights equal to those of citizens. Their language was Greek, and to varying degrees they adopted the culture of the polis. Powerful tensions resulted: between individuals or families of the Jewish community who were more and those who were less assimilated, within individuals, and between the Jewish community and Gentile residents.

One of the most thoroughly Greek of the Jewish authors we know from this period, Philo of Alexandria, dramatically exhibits the ambiguities of Diaspora life. Even he, thoroughly at home in the cultured world of the polis, recalls as something his readers will surely acknowledge that "God with a single call may easily gather together from the ends of the earth to any place that he wills the exiles dwelling in the utmost parts of the earth." Yet he cites this tradition only to use it as an analogy for a psychological observation, which he makes in the language of Hellenistic philosophy: in the same way reason can save a mind that has strayed and been abused by pleasure and lust.[2]

Rome was the dominant factor in any map of power in the first centuries of our era, and that held true for Jews of the Diaspora as for Palestinian Jews. Rome affected the two situations differently, however. In Judea, although in ordinary times the great majority of the population cooperated with the provincial authorities, whether grudgingly or enthusiastically, more and more came to resent the Romans as an occupying power. In the Diaspora cities, the more dangerous tensions were those which the Jews experienced with other groups. For example, in Alexandria the Jews were caught between the native Egyptians on the one hand and the Greek full citizens on the other. In those cases, Rome often appeared as an arbiter or even a patron.[3]

In the first and second centuries, a series of violent confrontations occurred, which left the situation of Jews in Palestine and in parts of the Diaspora permanently and severely altered. Rebellions against Roman rule in Palestine had flared up several times in the period of prefectural rule after Herod's death; late in the reign of Nero (A.D. 66), one of these exploded into a full-scale war of liberation. The rebellion was crushed by the Romans, though not without difficulty—it was not until 72 or 73 that they succeeded in overcoming the last holdouts in the fortress of Masada. Jerusalem was sacked and the Temple destroyed in 70, but the Jews were able to reorganize, creating new institutions and continuing both to exist and to exercise a certain degree of self-governance in the homeland. The results of the second revolt, in the time of Hadrian (A.D. 132–135), were more devastating. The Romans broke the resistance and killed the leader Simeon bar Kosiba—whom his followers called by the Messianic title "Bar Kochba," "Son of the Star." After that, they forbade Jews even to approach the site of the former Temple and, for a time, to circumcise their children or to study Torah. The Temple thereafter could function only as memory and symbol, not again as a present focus of identity. One response was the profound recasting of traditions and institutions that eventually produced, in the academies founded in villages of the Galilee and of Babylonia, what we now call "rabbinic Judaism."

The wars in Palestine had surprisingly little direct effect on Jews of the Diaspora. During the same period, however, there was a series of local but severe conflicts outside Palestine. In Alexandria in the year 38 the Roman prefect turned a blind eye to a series of mob attacks on the Jewish population. Appeals to the Roman emperor brought eventual relief, but no permanent solution to the underlying conflict. Early in the second century, under the emperor Trajàn, Jews revolted in Egypt and further west in cities of North Africa and on the island of Cyprus. Almost simultaneously revolts broke out also in portions of Mesopotamia under Roman rule. The Roman armies put down these revolts so ruthlessly that in portions of North Africa and Egypt the Jewish communities simply ceased to exist. Even then, however, Jews in other places were apparently unaffected. We have evidence, for example, of large, flourishing, and well-situated Jewish communities in Syria and in many places in western Asia Minor for centuries after these disasters.

If we inquire about the contexts within which the great moral traditions of Israel were interpreted, therefore, we must be sensitive both to the variety of different places and to the strong currents of change that were occurring precisely during the period in which the peculiar messianic sect that was to become Christianity was taking shape.

Some Representative Voices

It is no more possible to survey here the whole complex of Israel's traditions than it was to treat all of Greek and Roman philosophy. However, by listening to the classical words of lawgivers, priests, and prophets of Israel as they were retold by some representative voices in the Hellenistic and Roman periods, we will be able to some degree to discover how the traditions were understood in those times. Because it is important for us to understand the variety of

Judaisms at the beginning of our era, the samples that follow are deliberately quite diverse.

The Wisdom of Jesus the Son of Sira

Early in the second century B.C., before the crisis that led to the Maccabean uprising, a professional "scribe" in Jerusalem named Yeshua ben Sira (Jesus the son of Sira) wrote a book of "wisdom." "Wisdom" books were a familiar genre not only in Israel but throughout the ancient Near East; in the Hebrew Bible, Proverbs is the best-known example, but Ecclesiastes, Job, and certain psalms as well as portions of other books belong to the same type. Fifty or sixty years later Yeshua's grandson, who had moved to Egypt, probably Alexandria, in 132 B.C., translated the book into Greek. In Greek, too, it would have looked familiar, for it took the form of a collection of moral "sentences" or maxims (Greek *gnōmai*) of a wise teacher, and this was a kind of literature that had wide use in Greek and Roman moral instruction. Ben Sira's wisdom was of a sort well suited to cross cultural and geographical lines, as his grandson saw when he published it "for those living abroad who wished to gain learning, being prepared in character to live according to the law" (Prologue). At the same time, it is a wisdom peculiarly devoted to Israel's central traditions and institutions.[4]

Ben Sira speaks as a professional sage and teacher. At the end of the book he or someone else has added an acrostic poem (each line begins with a different letter of the Hebrew alphabet, though some have been lost) which recounts his long love affair with wisdom and invites students: "Draw near to me, you who are untaught, and lodge in my school" (51:23). Not everyone could afford this kind of instruction, as 38:24–39:11 makes plain. "The wisdom of the scribe depends on the opportunity of leisure; and he who has little business may become wise" (38:24). Farmers, smiths, and potters do work that is important, but it does not permit them to become *wise:*

> Without them a city cannot be established,
>   and men can neither sojourn nor live there.
> Yet they are not sought out for the council of the people,
>   nor do they attain eminence in the public assembly.
> They do not sit in the judge's seat,
>   nor do they understand the sentence of judgment;
> they cannot expound discipline or judgment,
>   and they are not found using proverbs.
>   (Sirach 38:32–33)

The "wisdom of the scribe" is thus a practical wisdom, intended like the Greek *paideia* to serve the public, political order. Ben Sira's grandson has emphasized the similarity by his translation, which speaks of the polis with its *boulē* and *ekklēsia*. The career that Ben Sira holds up for ambitious young men moves on a large scale:

> He will serve among great men
>   and appear before rulers;
> he will travel through the lands of foreign nations,
>   for he tests the good and the evil among men.
>
>   (39:4)

This picture is, to be sure, idealized. It corresponds to such legendary descriptions as that in the fictional *Letter of Aristeas,* [5] which tells how sages sent by the Jerusalem high priest to Alexandria entertained King Ptolemy Philadelphus by learned discourses at a banquet, before they began their assignment of translating the scriptures into Greek. Nevertheless, the notion of the scribe's role is not entirely unrealistic. In Ben Sira's time the authorities in Jerusalem, principally the high priest and his court, had to carry on delicate negotiations with the governments in Alexandria and in Antioch, as imperial fortunes shifted. Ben Sira and his students belonged to the circle of those who would be called upon for that kind of mission.

This circle is probably not identical with the powerful, wealthy families about whom we hear from other sources in Judea at that time. Chapter 13 is a collection of folk wisdom about the dangers of associating with rich people and about their immoral cunning.

> A rich man does wrong, and he even adds reproaches;
>   a poor man suffers wrong, and he must add apologies.
> A rich man will exploit you if you can be of use to him,
>   but if you are in need he will forsake you.
> If you own something, he will live with you;
>   he will drain your resources and he will not care.
>   • • • • • • • • • • • • • • • • • • •
> What peace is there between a hyena and a dog?
>   And what peace between a rich man and a poor man?
>
>   (13:3–5, 18)

Yet people like Ben Sira depend upon the patronage of those who hold wealth and power:

> A wise man advances himself when he speaks,
>   and a man of sense makes himself pleasant to the great.

> The man who tills his land heaps up a harvest,
> and he who pleases the great reaps pardon for his wrongdoing.
>
> (20:27–28, NEB)

Judging from his extravagant praise of Simon the high priest in chapter 50, Ben Sira himself was probably part of the Temple establishment, which had become the central governing structure in Judea. In particular, he must have been closely associated with the Oniad family of priests, who traced their line back to the Zadok installed by King David, and who were to lose their position to another powerful family in the struggles that brought on the Maccabean crisis.

Despite this dependence upon the powerful, Ben Sira retains the concern for the poor which was traditional in Israel and in much ancient Near Eastern wisdom.

> My son, do not cheat a poor man of his livelihood
> or keep him waiting with hungry eyes.
> Do not tantalize a starving man
> or drive him to desperation in his need.
> If a man is desperate, do not add to his troubles
> or keep him waiting for the charity he asks.
>
> (4:1–3, NEB)

The grandson's Greek has sharpened the admonition so that it is subtly different from ordinary Hellenistic attitudes toward the poor. Ben Sira had written, "My son, do not mock at *(la'ag)* the poor person's life." Here and in 34:20–21 the translator used the Greek word *aposterein,* "to cheat, defraud." Furthermore, he used the word *ptōchos,* which refers to a destitute person reduced to begging (as the context requires). In Hellenistic society the *ptōchos,* in contrast to the *penēs,* a person of modest means who had to work to earn his living, had no *rights* that could be "defrauded."[6] In Israel, however, there was a firm tradition, found not only in wisdom genres but also in the legal materials of the Torah and especially in the classical prophets, that God was especially the protector of the poor. God does not show favoritism toward the rich. Ben Sira, who lived in a society where, as we have seen, human beings who wanted to get ahead did have to kowtow to the rich, nevertheless remembers that God does not:

> He will not show partiality in the case of a poor man;
> and he will listen to the prayer of one who is wronged.
> He will not ignore the supplication of the fatherless,
> nor the widow when she pours out her story.
>
> (35:13–14)

The morality expressed in many of Ben Sira's maxims is prudential and commonsensical. Many of his sentences are in the form,
"Do not . . . , for . . . ," or the equivalent. "Do not quarrel with a
rich man, lest his resources outweigh yours." "Do not disdain a man
when he is old, for some of us are growing old." "Do not consult
with a fool, for he will not be able to keep a secret" (8:2, 6, 17).
"Wisdom" collects the accumulated experience of everyday life and
enables one to live better. The concluding poem says candidly, "Get
instruction with a large sum of silver, and you will gain by it much
gold" (51:28). Ben Sira has no qualms about slavery and strict
notions about how to keep the slaves in line: "Fodder and a stick
and burdens for an ass; bread and discipline and work for a servant"
(33:24). Although he later adds a more humane sentiment, "If you
have a servant, treat him as a brother, for as your own soul you will
need him," yet the motive seems more practical than philosophical:
"If you ill-treat him, and he leaves and runs away, which way will you
go to seek him?" (33:31).

Yet alongside these pragmatic rules for managing life stand statements of a theocentric ethic. The opening poem sounds a theme
that is pervasive in Hebrew wisdom literature: "All wisdom comes
from the Lord" (1:1), for "the Lord himself created her" (1:9). The
writer means something rather different from Plutarch's meditation
on the difference between God's being and human becoming as the
starting point of philosophy (above, p. 43). Like Solomon, Ben Sira
prays for the gift of wisdom, and receives it (51:13; cf. 39:6–11). He
is not necessarily referring to mystical illumination. On the one
hand, his most pragmatic observations are included, for "All things
are the works of the Lord, for they are very good" (39:16). On the
other, the scribe "devotes himself to the study of the law of the Most
High" (39:1). The book is in fact filled with direct and indirect
allusions to the Torah and other parts of scripture, to which Ben
Sira refers rather open-endedly as "the wisdom of all the ancients,
. . . prophecies, . . . the discourse of notable men, . . . parables,
. . . proverbs" (39:1b–3). Two generations later, the contours of
scripture were becoming more definite: "My grandfather Jesus,
after devoting himself especially to the reading of the law and the
prophets and the other books of our fathers . . . was himself also led
to write" (Prologue). Here is a theme that we shall hear again and
again in all kinds of Judaism in the Hellenistic and Roman eras:
scripture (becoming formally organized into the three parts, Torah,
Prophets, Writings) is the fountain of all wisdom. In the continual
interaction among scripture, reflection on Israel's history, and pres-

ent experience the Jew finds the ethical questions posed and the ethical directives given.

Ben Sira's ethic is theocentric in another way as well. Not only is God the giver of the wisdom that makes a good life possible and the authority who speaks through the scripture, God is also the guarantor of the moral reliability of the universe.

> Do no evil, and evil will never befall you.
> Stay away from wrong, and it will turn away from you.
> My son, do not sow the furrows of injustice,
> and you will not reap a sevenfold crop.
>
> (7:1–3)

Like the classical prophets of Israel, Ben Sira was able to discern the hand of God in the struggles between kingdoms, perhaps even the victory of the Seleucids over the Ptolemies in Palestine in his own time:

> Sovereignty passes from nation to nation
> on account of injustice and insolence and wealth.
> . . . .
> The Lord has cast down the thrones of rulers,
> and has seated the lowly in their place.
> The Lord has plucked up the roots of the nations,
> and has planted the humble in their place.
>
> (10:8, 14–15)

The sage is not so naive that he imagines that the good are always rewarded and the wicked punished immediately, yet he is sure that they will be in time. One must not be misled by appearances. The Lord may, for example, enrich the poor unexpectedly (11:12–13, 21). Even on one's deathbed reward or punishment may come: "Call no one happy before his death; a man will be known through his children" (11:27–28). If the notion that accounts might be squared after death had come to Ben Sira's attention, he did not embrace it (10:11; 17:27–32; 30:4–6). He holds to a moral structure of history that is essentially that taught by the book of Deuteronomy and by the biblical historical books written from the deuteronomic perspective. God tests but does not abandon those who trust in him. Ultimately, in this life, he will reward those who do his will and punish those who do not. As for his own people, bound to him in covenant, even his punishing is intended for correction, and their repentance finds his mercy ready.

Although the maxims of Ben Sira are addressed principally to the individual who is determined to be wise and good, it is the life of Israel that is the context of the admonitions. That means both the Israel of the biblical history and the present commonwealth, centered in the sacrifices and exalted priesthood of the Jerusalem Temple. It is from the biblical histories that Ben Sira draws his moral examples, both good and bad (16:6–10). Like some of the great "historical psalms" (78; 105; 106; 135; 136) his poems sum up the biblical account of God's creation of the world and of Israel and their moral significance (17:1–24). As his book progresses we hear more and more of the life of Israel and the Torah of God, until it climaxes in the "praise of famous men" of chapters 44–49 and the glorification of the current high priest in chapter 50. It is in Israel that wisdom is to be found. Wisdom's poem of self-praise (ch. 24) relates her wandering through the universe in search of a home (vs. 5–7)—a myth or metaphor found elsewhere as well, e.g., *1 Enoch* 42. In this case, however, Wisdom *does* find a resting place. The Creator of all things commands: "Make your dwelling in Jacob, and in Israel receive your inheritance" (vs. 8). The first part of this poem so strikingly resembles the hymns of Isis that were widely used in the Isis-Sarapis cult in the late Hellenistic and Roman periods that some scholars have argued Sirach 24 must be directly adapted from such a hymn.[7] Yet it climaxes with the statement, "All this is the book of the covenant of the Most High God, the law which Moses commanded us as an inheritance for the congregations of Jacob" (v. 23), followed by a series of allusions to the creation story of Genesis.

When Ben Sira set down in writing his lifetime's reflections, the cultured circles for whom he wrote were filled with excitement about the new wave of Hellenistic learning and institutions. There are many parallels between Ben Sira's observations and those of contemporary Greek philosophers and rhetoricians, and his grandson and translator would capitalize on some of those to make the book more accessible to the Greek-speaking Jews of Alexandria. Yet Ben Sira stood squarely against the assimilationist tendency of his "liberal" contemporaries.[8] His book breathes pride in the particularity of Israel's "eternal covenant" with the one Lord. To be wise for a Jew meant to become learned in Israel's scriptures, to keep the commandments, to remain loyal to the cultus of the Temple, to put one's trust in Israel's Lord who weighs all human deeds, rewarding the faithful and punishing the wicked. Between the time Ben Sira wrote and the time his grandson moved to Egypt, Judean society was torn apart by conflict between those who held such "conservative" views and those who wanted to exploit the opportunities of the new culture. We would like to know what Ben Sira's family was doing during those events and what the grandson thought of them in retrospect. He does not tell us. Yet he obviously thought the old-fashioned maxims of Yeshua would find a hearing among the hellenized Jews of Alexandria, though perhaps the phrases with which he qualified the intended audience, at the close of his prologue, are pointed: "for those living abroad who wished to gain learning, being prepared in character to live according to the law."

The Covenanters of Qumran

There were some in Israel who were much more deeply scarred by the events of the middle of the second century B.C. than Ben Sira's grandson appears to have been. Indeed, it was in those same circles around the old Zadokite priesthood that the disillusionment was especially profound. The son of the high priest Simon II, glorified in Sirach 50, was displaced and later murdered; Simon's grandson fled to Egypt and founded there a rival temple at the Jewish military colony of Leontopolis. The Jerusalem Temple suffered first the corruption of rivals for the high priesthood, then looting and desecration by the Syrian king. The success of the Maccabees in freeing the Temple and then the land from pagan domination added a heroic story and the new festival of Hanukkah to the enduring traditions of most Jews. Yet for some the fruit of victory quickly turned sour as this non-Zadokite family first took the high priesthood for themselves and then began to call themselves kings as well.

Among the disaffected was a small circle led by Zadokite priests who withdrew from Jerusalem and from ordinary life. In their eyes the world was in the grip of evil forces so powerful that it was naive to think that one could live happily and successfully in the world while remaining true to the eternal covenant, as Ben Sira had believed. Emigrating to the Diaspora, as Ben Sira's grandson did, or starting a new temple there, as Onias IV did, was an evasion. Only a "new planting" in Israel gave hope of purifying the holy land and the sanctuary. This group, "volunteers of God" or "devotees of Truth," withdrew to the wilderness near the western shore of the Dead Sea. After some twenty years during which "they were like blind men groping for the way," one of them wrote later, God "raised for them a Teacher of Righteousness to guide them in the ways of His heart" (CD 1.10–11).[9] They thus became a tightly organized "Community" of the "New Covenant."

It was this sect which, after nineteen centuries of oblivion, was dramatically revealed by the discovery of the now famous Dead Sea Scrolls. At the height of the Roman campaign against the Judean rebels, after A.D. 66, members of the group hid their library in the caves near their communal center, which was at a spot now called Khirbet Qumran. The Roman armies destroyed their settlement, and the precious leather rolls, some carefully protected in earthenware jars, others hastily stacked in the caves, lay untouched except by mold and worms until 1947. A chance discovery by a Bedouin goatherd led to years of intense exploration by Bedouin, archaeologists, and scholars to find, salvage, and read the manuscripts. Most scholars soon concluded that the sect belonged to the movement called the Essenes by Josephus, Philo, and other ancient writers. One of these writers, the pagan collector of curiosities Pliny the Elder, recorded that the major center of the Essenes was in a place that coincides with the mound of ruins, Khirbet Qumran. Excavated, the mound revealed an elaborate and self-sufficient settlement, something very like a monastery, which had flourished from the middle of the second century B.C. until A.D. 68.

The main outlines of the Qumran community's ethos will become clear if we look at just two of their documents. The first is a kind of constitution and by-laws of the sect. Its first modern editors called it "the Manual of Discipline"; now it is generally known by the words that appear in its first line, "Rule of the Community" (*serek ha-yahad*). A nearly complete copy (1QS) was found in Cave 1; fragments of other copies were found in Cave 4. The other document (CD) was first found early this century, far away from Qumran, in two imperfect medieval manuscripts in the storeroom of a very old synagogue in Cairo. It is similar in form to the Rule, but it legislates for a group "in the land of Damascus"—specialists still debate whether "Damascus," derived from Amos 5:27, is to be taken literally or as a symbolic name for the area of Qumran. Fragments found in the caves confirm the antiquity of the document of which the Cairo manuscripts are copies, and show that it was used at Qumran.

Both documents are written for people who live in a profoundly disordered world, and who see the roots of that disorder to be moral. They offer a prescription for a well-ordered life—indeed, for discovering the hidden and eternal order established by God. To attain that order, however, requires total dedication:

> All those who freely devote themselves to his truth shall bring all their knowledge, powers, and possessions into the Community of God, that they may purify their knowledge in the truth of God's precepts and

order their powers according to his ways of perfection and all their possessions according to his righteous counsel. (1QS 1.11–13)

It is no accident that "knowledge" stands first among the aspects of life that are to be devoted and transformed. The first task of those who "enter the covenant" is precisely to learn to understand the world in a different way. The "Rule of the Community" is addressed to "the master" or "instructor" *(maskîl)* and comprises the things he must teach the members.

> The Master shall instruct all the sons of light and shall teach them the nature of all the children of men according to the kind of spirit which they possess, the signs identifying their works during their lifetime, their visitation for chastisement, and the time of their reward.
>
> From the God of knowledge comes all that is and shall be. Before ever they existed he established their whole design, and when, as ordained for them, they come into being, it is in accord with his glorious design that they fulfill their work. The laws of all things are unchanging in his hand and he provides them with all their needs.
>
> He has created man to govern the world, and has appointed for him two spirits in which to walk until the time of his visitation: the spirits of truth and falsehood. Those born of truth spring from a fountain of light, but those born of falsehood spring from a source of darkness. All the children of righteousness are ruled by the Prince of Light and walk in the ways of light; but all the children of falsehood are ruled by the Angel of Darkness and walk in the ways of darkness. (1QS 3.13–21)

The violent disruptions which Judea had suffered were thus part of a universal struggle between suprahuman powers of good and evil. Armed with this secret knowledge, the initiate was prepared to make sense of events that seemed to mock such tidy moral expectations as those expressed by Ben Sira—to make sense, and to endure, for the struggle was not forever. God is in control of both good and evil powers and, "in the mysteries of his understanding, and in his glorious wisdom, God has ordained an end for falsehood [or, evil], and at the time of the visitation he will destroy it for ever" (1QS 4.18). Moreover, that time of visitation was very near, for the volunteers for the New Covenant believed themselves to belong to the generation of "the end of days."

If that is the way the world is, then to live wisely and rightly requires very specific action. It was time for those who belonged to the side of Light to withdraw from a society dominated by the forces of Darkness:

> They shall separate from the congregation of the men of falsehood and shall unite, with respect to the Law and possessions, under the

authority of the sons of Zadok, the Priests who keep the Covenant, and of the multitude of the men of the Community who hold fast to the Covenant. (1QS 5.1–3)

Both of our two documents are orders for persons who have chosen to "enter the Covenant" (1QS 1.8; 1.16–2.25; CD 2.2; 6.19; etc.), and the elaborate ceremony for doing that is based directly on the description in the book of Deuteronomy of the covenant made in the wilderness east of the Jordan under Moses' direction. The covenanters' own withdrawal to the desert of Judea was a deliberate evocation of that primordial stage of Israel's sacred history, and a fulfillment of prophecy:

> And when these become members of the Community in Israel according to all these rules, they shall separate from the habitation of ungodly men and shall go into the wilderness to prepare the way of HIM; as it is written, "Prepare in the wilderness the way of . . . ; make straight in the desert a path for our God" (Isa. 40:3). This (path) is the study of the Law [*midrash ha-torah*] which he commanded by the hand of Moses, that they may do according to all that has been revealed from age to age, and as the prophets have revealed by his Holy Spirit. (1QS 8.12–17)

Radical as their break was with the dominant institutions of Israel, and novel as many of their ideas sounded, yet the new covenanters saw themselves as restorers, not innovators. Although the knowledge they acquired was special, and the Master was ordered to "conceal the teaching of the Law from men of falsehood" and only to "impart true knowledge and righteous judgement to those who have chosen the Way" (1QS 9.17), yet this special knowledge was all to be found in the scriptures of Israel. To discover it, however, required inspiration and diligent searching *(midrash)*. For any group of the community having the minimal number of ten members, "there shall never lack a man among them who shall study the Law continually, day and night, concerning the right conduct of a man with his companion. And the Congregation shall watch in community for a third of every night of the year, to read the Book and to study Law and to pray together" (1QS 6.6–8).

It was apparently the anonymous "Teacher of Righteousness" who established the way in which the community reinterpreted biblical passages, for he was "the priest [in whose heart] God set [understanding] that he might interpret all the words of his servants the prophets, through whom he foretold all that would happen to his people and [his land]" (1QpHab 2.8–10). This last quotation is from one of a number of biblical commentaries of a peculiar kind that were found at Qumran. They show vividly how the members of the sect read the Bible as a collection of narratives, rules, and prophecies whose deepest meaning focused on the "final generation," to which they belonged. They saw their own experience cryptically predicted in scripture, and from scripture and reflection on the traditions of Israel's sacral history they drew the meaning of their experience and guidance for the ways they should now act. This interpretive activity was not random, for "the sons of Zadok," that is, the priestly leaders of the sect, were in charge (see, e.g., 1QS 5.9), and the discussion of the Torah in the plenary meetings of the congregation was strictly regulated (e.g., 1QS 6.8–13).

The ethos portrayed in these documents is radically sectarian. The fundamental ethical choice is whether to "enter the covenant," and that is virtually the same as the choice whether one is a child of Light or of Darkness. To be sure, the division does not exactly coincide with the boundaries of the community, for even within each child of Light there is some darkness and the Prince of Darkness leads him into sin: 1QS 3.21–24; 4.15f. Still, it is within the covenant that the aid of God and the Angel of Truth prevail. That is why the familiar traditions of Israel and even values shared by Israel with other peoples acquire an altered meaning within the context of the Essene world view.

For example, the Rule of the Community describes the road of goodness and the road of evil simply by listing virtues and vices: "a spirit of humility, patience, abundant charity, unending goodness, understanding, and intelligence . . ." over against "greed, and slackness in the search for righteousness, wickedness and lies, haughtiness and pride, falseness and deceit, cruelty and abundant evil, ill-temper and much folly and brazen insolence, abominable deeds (committed) in a spirit of lust, and ways of lewdness in the service of uncleanness, a blaspheming tongue, blindness of eye and dullness of ear, stiffness of neck and heaviness of heart . . ." (1QS 4.3, 9–11). A Ben Sira might have made a similar list, and so might a pagan moralist, perhaps calling up the familiar fable of Heracles at the crossroad, choosing the path of virtue or of vice.

Here, however, everything depends upon the context. For the Essenes the choice to enter a virtuous life is not available to everyone.

From the God of Knowledge comes all that is and shall be. Before ever they existed he established their whole design, and when, as ordained for them, they come into being, it is in accord with his glorious design that they fulfill their work. (1QS 3.15f.)

Nor is the pursuit of virtue a craft that can be mastered and whose reward is virtue itself. The all-encompassing virtue is obedience to the covenant and its goal is to stand approved at the "visitation" that God will bring to all humanity.

The ordinances that fill the latter portions of the Community Rule and the Damascus Covenant document thus hardly constitute a systematic ethic. They have to do with the way the community is to be organized and governed. They include very particular aspects of the relation of one member to another and of behavior in meetings. Yet the detailed rules are relatively few and far from being comprehensive legislation for all aspects of communal life. They must rather serve as examples and pointers, as reminders of the loyalty each member owes the community and of its extrordinary status as an island of purity in a defiled world.

> Whoever has borne malice against his companion unjustly shall do penance for six months/one year; and likewise, whoever has taken revenge in any matter whatever. Whoever has spoken foolishly: three months. Whoever has interrupted his companion whilst speaking: ten days. Whoever has lain down to sleep during an Assembly of the Congregation: thirty days. . . . Whoever has gone naked before his companion, without having been obliged to do so, he shall do penance for six months. Whoever has spat in an Assembly of the Congregation shall do penance for thirty days. (1QS 7.8–10, 12–13)

These rules, moreover, are temporary. Those who enter the covenant vow to accept governance by these "primitive precepts in which the men of the Community were first instructed until there shall come the Prophet and the Messiahs of Aaron and Israel" (1QS 9.11; cf. CD 12.22–13.1). This is emergency legislation for the "latter days." It is martial law of a very special sort, harking back to the ancient rules of Holy War, for the Remnant in Israel who prepare for the last great "War of the Sons of Light with the Sons of Darkness" (1QM). Within the community, there was continual study and debate to determine the way in which one ought to behave in face of the End (1QS 6.6–14). Yet the fundamental moral decision was whether to enter the community in the first place. There are passages in the later Damascus Rule that sound a bit more "worldly": rules for marriage and for the care of the poor, aged, sick, captives, and women without guardians (CD 14.12–16). Yet these merely point to this militant community's sense that it was the cadre of the true Israel; upon it alone rested the assignment to "prepare the way of HIM." This was the fiercely moral vision that flamed up in the fires set by Roman soldiers at Khirbet Qumran in A.D. 68—and faded in its ashes.

Philo

It would be hard to imagine a Jewish spokesman more different from the Qumran covenanters than Philo of Alexandria. He belonged to a wealthy and well-connected family; his father once lent to the future king Herod Agrippa, when the latter was in difficulties, a huge sum, with hardly a hope of getting it back. His nephew, Tiberias Julius Alexander, would become a Roman knight, procurator of Judea, and prefect of Egypt. We have already had occasion to note Philo's leadership—when the Jewish community of Alexandria sent a delegation to Gaius Caesar to complain about abuses —and some of his writings (above, p. 28).

Philo complains at times about the heavy weight of practical affairs that fell on his shoulders. Yet he found time to write a small library of books, many of which have survived. His major works are divided into three great series. The first, the "Exposition of the Law," begins with *The Creation of the World*, which ingeniously discovers Plato's metaphysics in the first two chapters of Genesis. Then the lives of the patriarchs are presented: they were "living laws" who embodied the principles of the divine law before the written code was given through Moses. Abraham, Isaac, and Jacob were subjects of three separate books, though the latter two have been lost. A *Life of Joseph* presents this figure, not as the scheming politician that Philo depicts in some other essays, but as a statesman, the ideal prefect of Egypt. *On the Decalogue* treats the Ten Commandments as a summary of the general principles upon which the whole law is based; *On the Special Laws* then lays out the application of these principles in the legislation found in the Pentateuch. *The Virtues* treats courage, humanity, repentance, and nobility, and *On Rewards and Punishments* summarizes the whole Exposition and adds, rather surprisingly, an eschatological conclusion. The Exposition presupposes that the reader also knows Philo's *Life of Moses*, so that can be regarded as the introduction to the whole.

The second series presents a luxuriant array of allegories of the stories of Genesis, beginning with chapter 2. Eighteen tracts are extant; at least nine have been lost. Finally, Philo wrote a systematic, verse-by-verse commentary on the greater part of the Pentateuch, in the form of questions and answers exploring the literal and the symbolic meaning of each biblical phrase. In the Greek, only quoted fragments have survived, and in Armenian only some sections of Genesis and Exodus. There are a few other miscellaneous works extant as well.[10] We will confine our attention here to the Exposition; a reading of at least the *Life of Moses,* the *Life of Abraham,* and the summary in *On Rewards and Punishments* is recommended.

It is clear from the arrangement of the Exposition that Philo saw in the Torah at least two things. First, it was the constitution for a utopia, a "Republic" *(politeia)* both older and better than Plato's. Second, it was a program of education *(paideia)*, the grandest and best anyone could imagine.

In order to discover these hidden powers in the books of Moses, one must learn to read them at several levels and from more than one perspective. To enable an interested but untrained reader to do that is the task Philo set himself—to initiate the inquirer (whether Jew or Gentile sympathizer) into "the lesser and the greater mysteries." First, this inquirer must recognize that there are three kinds of literature within the Pentateuch: cosmological, historical, and legislative (*On Rewards and Punishments* 1), and all are a necessary part of the training in virtue. Second, each portion may be read both "literally" and "allegorically." For example, at the literal level the story of Abraham is the account of a certain wise man coming to maturity through education. On the allegorical level, however, it is the progress of "a virtue-loving soul" (*Abraham* 68), i.e., it is universal. In Philo's allegories, characters, scenes, and events become symbols for virtues and vices or for metaphysical entities. Thus "symbolically the group of five cities" in the plain of Sodom and Gomorrah "is the five senses in us, the instruments of the pleasures which, whether great or small, are brought to their accomplishment by the senses" (*Abraham* 147).

What Philo finds in the Bible is thus a program of moral psychology. The human person is a combination of soul and body, and the soul itself is composite. Describing the composition, Philo can use Plato's description, or Aristotle's, or the Stoic, depending on what fits best the details of the text he is allegorizing.[11] Philo's picture of the world and of the human self is essentially Platonic; the structure of his ethics largely Stoic. It is a combination we find often in the intellectuals of the Roman period. In this vision, reason rules all. "The sole source and fountain of virtues" is "nature's right reason" (*Moses* 1.48)—a Stoic technical term, but for Philo the *logos* that pervades and gives order to all nature is not material, as in Stoicism, but spiritual and, indeed, a "power" of God. Although Philo often speaks of God in very personal terms, following the biblical texts, properly speaking the ultimate object of worship for him is beyond the personal powers that the Bible calls "God" and "Lord," beyond all appearances, even beyond the (Platonic) world of ideas that Reason apprehends. He is the One "to whom alone existence belongs." Plutarch would discover that truth in the inscription at Delphi (above, p. 43); Philo finds it in God's self-revelation to Moses, translated in the Septuagint, "I am the one who is" (Ex. 3:14; *Moses* 1.75). This source of all being is also source of all good. Infinitely far beyond the world, through his powers he nevertheless creates, sustains, and rules the world and is close to the soul that strives for wisdom and virtue. To be wise and good is, as for the Stoic, to "follow nature," but that means for Philo to draw near to God—to perceive the order that God created in the world, then to reason to the ruling and creating powers of God, ultimately to the unitary Reason of God, and then, beyond even rational apperception, to unite with the One Who Is. The name "Israel" for Philo, by an ingenious but incorrect etymology, means "the man who sees God" (e.g., *On Rewards and Punishments* 44).

How does one become wise and virtuous? Three factors are important: nature (that is, the individual's innate capacities), education, and practice. The three are represented respectively by the patriarchs Isaac, Abraham, and Jacob; Moses combines all three (e.g., *Moses* 1.76; *On Rewards and Punishments* 24–56). All this is quite familiar in pagan philosophical ethics (see, for example, Pseudo-Plutarch, *On the Education of Children*). Describing Moses' childhood education, Philo imagines that he received, with some special additions, the education that any aristocratic citizen of Alexandria would want for his sons (*Moses* 1.21–24). It is very likely the same kind of education that Philo himself received.

Nevertheless, it is a far from trivial fact that Philo expounds his universal program of moral education, not in philosophical essays or Socratic dialogues, but in ornately detailed commentary on the text of the Pentateuch. His interpretations are, to our taste, often arbitrary, even fantastic. Nevertheless, if we read attentively, we discover in almost every instance that there is some specific starting point in the words of the Greek text, or in the combination of two parallel texts, that provides the springboard of his allegorical gymnastics. He is fully as convinced as any disciple of the Teacher of Righteousness at Qumran that all essential moral truth is to be found in the words of Moses (unlike the Essenes, he makes little use of the other parts of the Bible to interpret the Torah).

Consequently, we would completely misunderstand Philo if we read him merely as a clever Platonist, teaching his fellow Jews to assimilate to the dominant culture. "Israel" may be in Philo's uni-

versalizing moral allegories any virtuous soul who progresses toward the vision of God, but at the same time Israel is the organized
politeuma of Alexandrian Jews, over which God watches and whose
persecutors he will punish (the moral of *On Flaccus* and *The Embassy
to Gaius*). Israel is "the most God-loved nation," which received
priesthood and prophecy on behalf of humankind (*Abraham* 98),
which makes intercession for all humanity (*Moses* 1.149). If the
greatest of the Greek philosophers have arrived at a vision of reality
very like what Philo finds in scripture, that is no surprise. Abraham
had already discovered God's law by contemplating nature; the
order of nature is the same as the order of nature's Creator (*Abraham*
61, 88). What the same Creator revealed through his prophet Moses
must therefore be the same moral order that nature reveals to the
wise.

Philo's ethic is therefore not an ethic of Jews who will assimilate
into the high culture of Alexandria, but of those who, like himself,
want to be at home in both worlds. They embrace the Greek peda-
gogical and philosophical tradition and find a splendid harmony of
values between it and the scripture of Israel. They accept the political order of the Roman empire and believe that it can be reformed
if virtuous men hold power. The Greek polis is the arena in which
they want to live their public lives. Yet at the same time they proudly
insist on the integrity of the Jewish community. Philo has only
disdain for those Alexandrian Jews who, like himself, find the real
meaning of the biblical commandments to be symbolic and who,
unlike him, discard the literal practice of such rules as circumcision.
Such people, he says, want to be bodiless souls, living in a desert
not in a community (*The Migration of Abraham* 89–93). In the descendants of Jacob who sojourned in Egypt he sees an analogy to
the situation of the "resident aliens" of his own community, "who
are anxious to obtain equal rights with the burgesses and are near
to being citizens" (*Moses* 1.35). He has harsh words for those who,
when they prosper, "look down on their relations and friends and
set at naught the laws under which they were born and bred, and
subvert the ancestral customs . . . by adopting different modes of
life" (*Moses* 1.31)—like his nephew Tiberias Alexander? On the
other hand, he speaks very favorably of proselytes. The Judaism he
portrays really is a universal culture. His Moses is, like Adam, a
"citizen of the world" (*kosmopolitēs; Moses* 1.157; *Creation of the World*
142). Moses begins his legislation with an account of creation to
teach "that the world is in harmony with the Law, and the Law with
the world, and that the man who observes the law is constituted

thereby a loyal citizen of the world, regulating his doings by the purpose and will of nature, in accordance with which the entire world itself also is administered" (*Creation of the World* 3). Nevertheless, Moses is and remains "the legislator of the Jews."

In Ben Sira we found that the old deuteronomic view of history was still alive: the belief that God guides the course of history—especially as it affects his chosen people Israel—to moral ends, ultimately punishing the wicked and rewarding the faithful. The Qumran community formed around a radical version of that vision of history, which they believed would reach its climax in their own time. In Philo we hear only muted echoes of the deuteronomic conception of the moral purpose of history, but it is not entirely lacking. He concludes his "Exposition of the Law," for example, with a tract *On Rewards and Punishments*. In it he describes the historical part of the Pentateuch as "a record of good and bad lives and of the sentences passed in each generation on both, rewards in one case, punishments in the other" (*On Rewards and Punishments* 2). And, while he tends to psychologize and individualize these examples, nevertheless Philo clearly believes that Israel as a people has its special history, its God-given mission, and its rewards and punishments and protection by God.

The Rabbis of the Mishnah

With the destruction of the Temple in Jerusalem in the year 70, the remaining institutional center of Israel was gone. Scribes, the successors of professionals like Ben Sira, had continued to refine their study of scripture and to compile the practical wisdom of the ages, the guidelines from scripture, reason, and experience to the will of God for his people. But the supporting structures of their life were all connected to the Temple, and it was now lost. A few in Israel, scribes, priests, and lay loyalists to the line of "Zadok," had long before abandoned the Temple and prepared in the desert for the last, angelic, cleansing war. But it had not come in the way they imagined, and now their Community of the New Covenant was also destroyed.

Outside the land of Israel, the disorientation was not so complete. For people like Philo and his readers, who had learned to make their peace with the cosmopolitan culture of the Greek cities and with the politics of Rome, the destruction of the Temple was doubtless a cause for profound sorrow. Yet it did not much affect their daily lives or alter the ways they maintained their identity as Jews. Some of them would face their own trials by war in times to come, but many would continue to live in relative peace and to flourish, centuries later. Nevertheless, the far future of Judaism did not rest with them.

Instead, the foundations were being laid for a different way for Israel to define and maintain itself, a way that has proved itself tough beyond what anyone could then have imagined to survive vast cultural changes, in good times and terrible times, until the present age. The founders are almost entirely hidden by our ignorance of Palestinian life between the first revolt against the Romans and the second. Tradition has it that a professional sage named Yohanan ben Zakkai, one of those successors of Ben Sira's class, gained permission of the Romans, when Jerusalem was under its final siege, to start a school. He chose for its site the village called Jamnia by the Romans and Yavneh in Hebrew. He and his pupils called themselves "rabbis," and "rabbinic" Judaism was born in their efforts to combine old traditions, careful study of scripture, and daring innovations into a program for Israel's continuing life.[12]

It is possible to reconstruct, from later documents, something of the accomplishment of Yohanan and his colleagues and pupils, but the results are fragmentary and uncertain. One reason for the dimness of our historical vision is that the devastation of the Bar Kochba revolt and its aftermath, already mentioned, came in between Yavneh's beginnings and the formation of those documents and institutions which have survived. The fog begins to lift only about two generations after Bar Kochba, that is, around A.D. 200, when what was to become the foundation document of later "normative" Judaism was compiled: the Mishnah. Thus the completed Mishnah stands this side of the birth of the Christian movement by about as many years as the Wisdom of Jesus ben Sira stands on the other. For that reason alone it would form a fitting place for our survey of Israel's Great Traditions to conclude. The more important reason is that the Mishnah brings into the light a way of construing Israel's ethos which, however obscure its long prehistory remains, would profoundly shape the most enduring of the several ways Israel would approach the future.

Of all the documents we have looked at in this chapter, the Mishnah will seem the most opaque to a reader who has not studied it previously. We open an English translation[13] and discover that the first of its six major divisions is called *Zera'im,* the Hebrew word for "seeds." "Seeds" in turn is divided into sections, the first of which is called "Blessings," the second "Corner" *(Peah).* "Corner" is a curious title, so we dip into it. First, we are told that "corner" is one of several things "for which no measure is prescribed." The next paragraph, however, makes up that lack:

> *Peah* should be not less than one-sixtieth part [of the harvest]. And although they have said that no measure is prescribed for *Peah,* it should ever accord with the size of the field and the number of the poor and the yield [of the harvest].

We cannot make sense of this unless we know some things which the text does not tell us. In this case, the puzzle is not hard to solve. The laws of scripture command a farm owner to leave a corner of a field unreaped so that poor people can come and harvest the produce there (Lev. 19:9–10; 23:22). The Bible does not say how big a "corner" is, however, so the Mishnah specifies that. Nor does scripture say what kinds of crops are subject to the rule, so Mishnah will explain that, too:

> Whatsoever is used for food and is kept watch over and grows from the soil and is all reaped together and is brought in for storage is liable to the law of *Peah*. Grain and pulse come within this general rule. Among trees, sumach, carob, walnut trees, almond trees, vines, pomegranate trees, olive trees, and palm trees are subject to the law of *Peah*. (*Peah* 1.4–5)

We see at once that the framers of the Mishnah, and the traditions on which they drew, were seriously concerned about the moral code found in the Bible. Like Ben Sira, they understand the biblical theme that God cares about the poor and holds his people responsible for their protection. The remaining portions of the tractate *Peah* deal similarly with other problems of this and other biblical rules about the rights of the poor. In addition, the Mishnah's authorities set limits that are designed to prevent abuse of these rules, for example by those who may not really be poor, and to protect the small farmer. There is a refreshing matter-of-factness about the way they fill in loopholes and pin down ambiguities. They are talking about real wheat and olives and actual poor persons. No allegories here of Platonic psychology, no cryptic references to the Poor as the Sons of Light in the Last Days, not even Ben Sira's elegant aphorisms.

Not all of Mishnah's puzzles are so easy to solve, however. If we turn to the last of the Mishnah's divisions, called "Purities," which is also the longest, most complex, and probably oldest part,[14] we find, for example:

> [As to] vessels of wood, and vessels of leather, and vessels of bone, and vessels of glass—when they are flat, they are clean [insusceptible of receiving uncleanness], and when they form receptacles, they are [sus-

ceptible of becoming] unclean. [If] they are broken, they are clean. [But immersion will also purify them]. [If] one went and made of them [the sherds] [new] vessels, they receive uncleanness from now and henceforth. (*Kelim* 2.1)[15]

The translator has made things easier for us by adding the words within brackets; without them, the language is as terse as the notes we might jot down while listening to a lecture. The Mishnah is obviously written for people who know a great deal about its subject already—and this time what they know cannot be learned simply by closely reading scripture. To be sure, the roots of the system of Purities are in scripture: "You shall keep the people of Israel separate from their uncleanness, lest they die in their uncleanness by defiling my tabernacle that is in their midst" (Lev. 15:31). The Mishnah, however, has developed a whole calculus of clean and unclean and the ways in which people and things move between the one category and the other:

[As to] the smallest [size] of earthenware vessels: "Their [rimmed] bottoms or their sides [which can] sit without supports [are unclean if] their measure is [=if they hold] as much [oil as needed for] anointing a small [finger of a child]. [And this measurement applies to vessels which, when whole, hold] up to a *log*. [If, when whole, such vessels held] from a *log* to a *se'ah*, [the uncleanness will persist if the remnant may hold] a quarter-*log*. . . ."—the words of R. Ishmael. R. 'Aqiva says, "I for my part do not place on them a measure. But [as to] the smallest size of clay vessels—their bottoms and their sides [which can] sit without supports—their measure is as much [oil as needed for] anointing a small [finger of a child]. [And this measure applies to all vessels up] to small cooking pots. From small cooking pots to Lydian jars [the uncleanness will persist if the remnant may hold] a quarter-*log*. " (*Kelim* 2.2)[16]

The calculus is difficult, and we are told of great authorities who have solved its problems in different ways. Who needs to know all this, and much, much more that is similar, and why?

The framers of the Mishnah prefaced the details of Purities with several climactic lists that serve as hints to the theoretical context. The pair of lists in 1.5–9 is most revealing. The former lists ten degrees of uncleanness, ranging from "he whose atonement [sacrifice] is incomplete," and therefore is not permitted to eat Holy Things but can eat Heave Offering, through several ways of becoming polluted by bodily fluids, through leprosy, to the potency of a dismembered limb to pollute. The second list is of "ten degrees of holiness," beginning with "The land of Israel is holier than all [other] lands." Then, in ascending order of holiness and in concentric circles: walled cities, Jerusalem, the Temple Mount, the rampart of the Temple, the court of women, the court of Israel, the court of the priests, the area between porch and altar, the sanctuary, the Holy of Holies. The differences between the stages are specified in terms of the level of impurity that prevents a person from entering each. Thus "holiness" and "impurity" are reciprocal concepts. Together they establish a sharply focused, stable world, at the center of which are Jerusalem, the Temple, the Holy of Holies.

Yet this center, when the Mishnah was compiled, had been destroyed. Is the definition of holiness here only an exercise in nostalgia? How is the matter-of-factness with which details of purity are sorted out to be reconciled with the artifice of a world focused on a center that does not exist?

The link between the two is an interpretive step that was apparently taken long before, which the Mishnah does not describe but takes for granted. Someone—most scholars think it was the sect of the Pharisees—had hit upon the revolutionary idea that the kind of purity that the Bible required for participation in the Temple's cultus ought to be embodied in the home of every Jew. The Qumran sect had organized around a similar concept of purity, but they thought it could be realized only in the desert, in a community of volunteers who removed themselves from the polluted city and Temple, until a last war of angels and men should cleanse the land. The Pharisees, on the contrary, made themselves a pure sect in the midst of the people, and the rabbis after them wanted the table of every Jew's home to have the holy centrality, protected by the concentric barriers against impurity, that the now-lost altar of the Temple had had.

Thus, while the symbolic center of the universe remains the remembered and idealized Temple, the practical center of the Mishnah's concerns is the ordinary home of a Jew in Israel. Jacob Neusner describes it in this way:

> The Mishnah knows about all sorts of economic activities. But for the Mishnah the center and focus of interest lie in the village. The village is made up of households, each a unit of production in farming. The households are constructed by, and around, the householder, father of an extended family, including his sons and their wives and children, his servants, his slaves, the craftsmen to whom he entrusts tasks he does not choose to do. The concerns of householders are in transactions in land. . . . The principal transactions to be taken up are those of the householder who owns beasts which do damage or suffer it; who harvests his crops and must set aside and so by his own word and deed

sanctify them for use by the castes scheduled from on high; who uses or sells his crops and feeds his family; and who, if he is fortunate, will acquire still more land.[17]

In the Mishnah's world not much changes, except the daily round from recital of the "Hear, O Israel" on rising to the same in the evening, the weekly arrangements from Sabbath to Sabbath, the moon's cycles and women's periods, the seasons of nature and of the appointed festivals. Like the Fiddler on the Roof, the point in village life is to keep one's balance. Balance is the aim of all commercial transactions, as the rules found mostly in the fourth division make clear. In case of doubt, one ought always to follow the practice that prevails in the place where one is. When two persons exchange goods either by barter or by sale, neither should end up richer or poorer than before. As was the case almost always in ancient societies, the villager saw the goods of life as distinctly limited. If one person got more than his share, someone else must have less: life is a zero-sum game. The game is played through a continual round of exchanges, whose goal is something very like the proportional equity that Aristotle defined. Like Aristotle, too, the Mishnah's rabbis begin with what good men—landowning heads of households—in stable communities already do. Where Aristotle aims at the clear, logical statement of the general principle, however, the rabbis pursue the individual instance and the thinkable exceptions. They rarely generalize; they exemplify. The scale of their ethos is very small.

What has become of history in the Mishnah? Where is that recurring theme of human communities called to account by God which we found in the old deuteronomic histories, still in Ben Sira's wisdom and even hidden away among Philo's allegories, and elevated to a glorious scenario of judgment at the end of days, in the Qumran texts? This motif is not entirely missing from the Mishnah. For example, *Sanhedrin* 10 lists various groups, mostly in the biblical narratives but some contemporary, who "have no share in the world to come." Yet this discussion is isolated and marginal. Of course the Mishnah's rabbis believe that God's judgment will ultimately settle all questions of justice. Surely they expect that Elijah will come to put disputed points at rest, and God will reveal an Anointed King to bring an age of peace and justice. Yet for now the decisions are given into human hands. Human study and reason determine the boundaries; human actions make things pure or impure. Time is filled with the cycle of day, week, and seasons. Those beliefs that the last days were at hand, when Israel's armies would join the hosts of heaven to purify the land, twice within less than a century had fed armed revolt in Judea, followed by devastating loss. The Mishnah's silence about such things speaks eloquently.

Recurring Themes

It is as impossible as it would be misleading to summarize *the* ethos represented by the several documents we have looked at. The variety that is evident in them is too serious to permit homogenization. Philo praises the Essenes, but makes them a model of Greek philosophical virtues. It is doubtful whether the Essenes of Qumran would have regarded him as a model of anything except an Israelite captured by the Prince of Darkness. Yet both saw themselves as faithful to the divine covenant. The diversity is not surprising, for these documents span four centuries of Jewish life, in several places and several quite different social and cultural settings, and separated in time by more than one political disaster. Yet one of the purposes of our survey was simply to confront that diversity, because even now some accounts of early Christian ethics assume that "Judaism" in the first century was one thing. It was not.

Nevertheless, there are a few themes which have turned up frequently in these sources, and it may be useful to recall them. We must be careful, however, not to think that such a list constitutes the profile of any real Jewish community in antiquity.

The Moral Structure of History

In the Hebrew Bible there are many variations on one major theme: God guides the course of history—at least as it affects his chosen people Israel—to moral ends, ultimately punishing the wicked and rewarding the faithful. The classical prophets of the eighth through the sixth centuries B.C. articulated and enlarged this conviction in manifold ways. In a more schematic fashion it forms the leitmotif of Deuteronomy and of the narratives of Israel's and Judah's history that were composed under the influence of the deuteronomic ideology. In the Hellenistic and Roman eras, divers circles of Judaism still believed that all human activities stand under God's judgment. Even so placid and worldly a wisdom as that taught by Yeshua ben Sira firmly asserted that God gives every person his just deserts, here in this life and in his own time. Those who labored to comprehend the defeats and dislocations that shook Judea after

Ben Sira's time turned more and more often to the notion of some
final, cataclysmic settling of accounts. Only in the Mishnah, compiled when memories of the Bar Kochba debacle were fresh, have
we found eschatological hopes muted and questions about history
pushed to the periphery of attention. Writing near the turn of the
first century, Josephus reaffirmed the deuteronomic vision as the
moral of his own largest work, *The Jewish Antiquities:*

> The main lesson to be learnt from this history by any who care to
> peruse it is that men who conform to the will of God, and do not
> venture to transgress laws that have been excellently laid down, pros-
> per in all things beyond belief, and for their reward are offered by God
> felicity; whereas, in proportion as they depart from the strict observ-
> ance of these laws, things (else) practicable become impracticable, and
> whatever imaginary good thing they strive to do ends in irretrievable
> disasters.[18]

Now the notion that history teaches morals was a commonplace
in Greco-Roman rhetoric and historical writing. Harold Attridge
has shown that Josephus' own "moralizing history" was dependent
in this as in other respects on pagan models, especially Dionysius
of Halicarnassus' *Roman Antiquities.*[19] Yet the theocentrism of the
Jewish moralizing historians, however widely their accounts differ
from one another, distinguishes them from the pagan authors who
treat such themes. Of course the pagan histories are not infrequently punctuated by the intervention of the gods, and not a few
orators assured the leaders of Rome that they could not have gained
such power without the gods' favor. What was special to the historical conception held by many Jews was the notion that there is but
one God with power to determine finally all human affairs, judging
all by transcendent standards and showing no partiality. This is not
to say that only Jews believed in one God transcending all other
beings; many pagans, in various ways, believed that. Nor is it to say
that all Jews believed that there was only one divine being; most
Jews like most pagans believed there were a great many, of various
ranks, some good some bad, whom they called angels (i.e., "messengers"). Pagans called them "gods" and *daimones*. What made
Jewish monotheism unique—and difficult for other people in
Roman pluralist society to understand—was the social embodiment
of their belief. One God alone must be worshiped; the cults of all
others must be shunned. The exclusivity of cult corresponds to the
boundaries of the Jewish communities as resident aliens in the cities
of the empire. *Their* God was the one God, and *he* would reward and
punish all alike by his unquestionable standards of virtue.[20]

The People Israel

The social correlate to the belief in one God is the one people of God, Israel. Given the diversity of Jewish identities that we find in the Roman era, to be sure, we may want to say that its oneness is only a mental construct. There was no single institution that embodied or represented Israel. Nevertheless, it is not an empty paradox to say that the variety of attempts to embody Israel's uniqueness itself attests to the power of the symbol. Whether it is the Qumran volunteers, reenacting the wilderness rituals of Deuteronomy to establish anew the broken covenant, or Philo insisting that only "the nation that sees God" was therefore able before anybody else to perceive the madness of Caligula's delusions of divinity, or the Mishnah's rabbis meticulously calculating the logic of the holy things that could no longer be offered in a temple that no longer stood—for all there are graces given and obligations imposed on this people because they are Israel. Whether in the villages of Galilee or the markets and courts of Alexandria, they found or invented ways to remain Israel—however much involved in the common world around them, still distinctive, separate.

Scripture

All varieties of Jewish community for which we have evidence from the Roman era assign to scripture a special place among their norms. As far as we can tell from our present knowledge of groups in the Roman world, this is a unique characteristic of the Jewish ethos. Of course there were classics of pagan literature, beginning with Homer, which every educated person in the world of Greco-Roman culture learned, and pagan moralists quoted them incessantly as illustrations of moral lessons. And there were Jews who used the Bible that same way. There were also distant parallels in some of the philosophical schools' study of their founders' works. Yet the sources we have looked at, and countless others, accord to the Torah of Moses, at least, a status far beyond that ordinarily attributed to Homer or to Plato, or even to the sayings of Pythagoras or of Epicurus by their respective disciples. Here the eternal wisdom of God can be found. There are also, of course, sacred books in most religious traditions of antiquity, and there was widespread curiosity about them among many intellectuals of the Roman empire. So far as we can discover, however, these generally provided only rather narrowly specialized directives or lore pertaining to the tasks of priests and other functionaries. There was nothing like the constitutional status that the Torah had in Jewish communities.

Further, there is quite early evidence that for many Jews "the scriptures" meant a specific, limited group of writings whose extent had been fixed "of old." Writing around A.D. 100, Josephus says, "We do not possess myriads of inconsistent books, conflicting with each other. Our books, those which are justly accredited, are but two and twenty, and contain the record of all time." His list is probably equivalent to the list of twenty-four books found in later Talmudic authorities. He divides them into three groups: five books of Moses, the prophets, and "four books [of] hymns to God and precepts for the conduct of human life."[21] Some two hundred years earlier Ben Sira's grandson had spoken of "the law, the prophets, and the other books," without naming or numbering them. Not all Jews agreed on the extent of the list; the Qumran community, for example, evidently gave authority to a number of writings that are not included in Josephus' canon. Further, it may be misleading to speak of a Jewish "canon" in this period, for that is a later, Christian term, and to use it may impose an alien category on the early evidence. Nevertheless, it is apparent that an identifiable corpus of scriptures, including preeminently the five books attributed to Moses, had a constitutive role in Jewish ethical discourse.[22]

Law

How the scriptures bear upon ethical decisions was a question about which different Jewish communities had a wide range of different ideas, as the samples above should have made obvious. All of them, however, talk in one way or another about "law" and "commandments." There are obvious and not-so-obvious reasons for that. For one thing, the Roman provincial administrators, when times were tranquil, gave a degree of self-government to recognizable *ethnē*, "nations," and to organized immigrant groups from such *ethnē* in the cities. The traditional laws of such communities became the basis for this limited autonomy. Thus Julius Caesar and his successors, as Josephus is careful to point out, recognized the "ancestral laws" of the Jews.[23] There was therefore a certain incentive to codify the rule-like aspects of scripture and tradition and to construe them as law. On the other hand, it is obvious that the Torah does contain codes of law of certain kinds, and these were manifestly extended and elaborated by scribal activity and by the practice of local courts not only in the land of Israel but also in Diaspora communities.

To call the ethics of the various Jewish communities a "legal" or "nomistic" ethic, however, runs the risk of serious distortion. One problem is a matter of language. In the sources quoted above, "law" often translates Torah, which was frequently already translated into Greek by the ancient writers as *nomos.* The trouble is that *torah* is much broader than *nomos* and *nomos* is broader than "law." The other major problem is that Christian scholars, especially Protestants, have for generations used "legalism" as a pejorative term to describe a theory of salvation attributed to Judaism, from which Christians were supposedly liberated, particularly by the teachings of Paul. In this century we have come to see that this picture is wrong in many ways. Luther's polemics against the penitential system of the late medieval church has been projected onto Paul's polemics against the "Judaizing" apostles of Galatia, and the Lutheran Paul's polemical statements have been taken as historical description of "Judaism." And then post-industrial-revolution individualism has been read into all of them. The resultant layers of distortion cannot be untangled here.[24]

The way to escape from the thicket of misunderstandings is by asking rigorously the question, What were the functions of laws, rules, and commandments in the various circles of Jewish life around the time Christianity began? That question, too, is the fitting subject for a book of its own, or several. There are only a few observations that we can make before leaving this topic. First, most Jews agreed that God had given very specific commandments to his people and that the premier way in which one proved faithful was by obeying them. Second, the contexts in which the ancient sources talk about such obedience only rarely allude to what Christians call "personal salvation." The late first-century apocalypse called *Fourth Ezra,* which we have not looked at, comes closest to treating this problem. Third, where any explicit reasons for obeying the commandments are stated or can be deduced, they have to do with making the community into the sort of people that God wants it to be. That Jewish ethics are communal ethics is one generalization that our sources will warrant. Even the writers who wanted to construe the Torah in the most universal terms possible, like Ben Sira and Philo, come back to the issue of Israel's special privileges and obligations. Fourth, those examples of rule collections that we have looked at—the "ordinances" of the Qumran Community Rule and the Damascus Rule, the *halakah* of the Mishnah—comprise a peculiar kind of law. Even the Mishnah, as diverse and wide-ranging as are the topics of its six divisions, by no means constitutes a code regulating all aspects of behavior. Nor can the commandments it singles out be taken as *the* test cases by which a Jew's "salvation" stands or falls. Rather, it only treats some debatable points, exemplary and emblematic of a vast, complex world view. The austere scholarship of the Mishnah examines the logic of holiness. Yet the premises for analysis of the debated points are selected both from the commandments of the Torah and from the common practice of the faithful village householder. The commandments are signals more than legislation. Perhaps this is true of most ancient law, including the biblical codes themselves.[25]

What the sources say about "law" in early Judaism thus ranges between two widely separated poles. At one pole God's law, that is, the Torah, comprises what we might call the meaningful structure of the universe—not merely the human universe but all that is real. Ben Sira would find in it the very Wisdom of God. Philo would discover the rational constitution governing all of nature, for which he uses the Stoic terms "right reason" and "nature's law." At the other pole are the specific commandments that the Jew performs to signal to himself and others that he is a child of the Covenant. The list is not uniform; what the Essene at Qumran must do each day, to keep his standing in that community, is very different from what Philo would do in Alexandria. Yet for both the doing is essential. To follow the nonobservant allegorists, Philo argues, is like wanting to be without a body and without a human community. Thus again we find self-consciousness about the community. In the age of the classical prophets and legislators of Israel, before the Babylonian exile, the existence of the nation could be taken for granted. The issue was how the nation could be just. In all the subsequent ages, Israel's existence itself was in question. The first point in each form of the variety of Jewish ethics, therefore, is to *be* Israel.

4

The Christian Communities

Stalking the early Christians, we draw concentric circles. In the world of the Greek-varnished culture of the eastern Mediterranean, transformed by the power and order of Rome, the Jewish communities of homeland and Diaspora were a special case. Within the manifold adaptations of Judaism to that larger world, the small circle of Jesus' followers appeared, spread, and quickly became multiform itself. The meaningful world in which those earliest Christians lived —the world which lived in their heads as well as that which was all around them—was a Jewish world. But the Jewish world was part of the Greco-Roman world. If therefore we are looking for some "pure" Christian values and beliefs unmixed with the surrounding culture, we are on a fool's errand. What was Christian about the ethos and ethics of those early communities we will discover not by abstraction but by confronting their involvement in the culture of their time and place and seeking to trace the new patterns they made of old forms, to hear the new songs they composed from old melodies.

The classical polis, as we saw in chapters 1 and 2, was first the practical and then the theoretical context of the great ethical traditions of Greece. The complex ethical issues confronting anyone who, informed by those traditions, wished in the first century of our era to achieve the classical goal of the well-wrought life were different from those of Aristotle's time, because the polis itself was different. So, too, the ethical imperatives of the Jews, revolving around the two poles of the one God and his one people, were transformed as the forms of Israel's communal life were altered and diversified (chapters 1 and 3). In order to understand the moral formation of the emerging Christian groups, it is not enough to investigate their appropriation of or reaction to those great traditions. First we must ask about their social forms. Where did they stand within the world of the cities of the Roman empire? What were their relationships with the other groups and movements in Judea and Galilee? With the Jewish communities of the Diaspora?

In this chapter we will look at the shapes of the early Christian communities, first in the setting of their origin in the land of Israel, then in the arena of their rapid spread, the cities of the eastern Roman provinces. In the next chapter, we will undertake to discern some of the patterns of meaning in the ways they talked and behaved, the "grammar" of early Christian morality.

A Messianic Sect in Israel

Christianity began as a sect of Judaism, in the villages of Judea and Galilee. This statement is a commonplace in modern scholarship, and it makes several important points. However, we need to be careful about what we mean by "sect," and to keep in mind that "Judaism" in the first century was a number of complicated things.

Sect

When modern sociologists, beginning with Max Weber and Ernst Troeltsch, began using the category "sect," it was to define a type of religious association the opposite of the "church." In ancient society, however, there was no organization remotely like the church that would evolve in late medieval and Reformation Europe, and the latter was the starting point for Weber and Troeltsch. When we speak of early Christianity as a sect of Judaism, we must accordingly recognize that we are using the term in an extended sense. "Judaism" was not a "church." To call early Christianity a sect means that it was a deviant movement within a cohesive culture that was defined religiously (in our sense of the word). The Christian movement understood itself in terms of the great traditions of that locally dominant culture—both positively and negatively. It was "sectarian" because the organizing center of the group's identity consisted in a constellation of beliefs and patterns of behavior that was not, as a whole, shared by other groups of Jews. It was those beliefs and that kind of behavior that determined who the Christians were, and not the great institutions of Israel—Temple, priesthood, professional interpreters of scripture—even though the latter might be presupposed, and the attitudes toward them by various groups of Christians might vary. Thus the early believers in Jesus the Messiah have to be compared with other identifiable movements or sects of Jews, such as the Essenes, the Pharisees, and the Therapeutae. Like them, the Jesus movement presupposed the great traditions of Israel and many of the common interpretive procedures and institutions, yet it interpreted those traditions, used those procedures, and responded to those institutions in deviant—sometimes radically deviant—ways. Like the other Jewish sects, it drew the boundaries of the sacred community differently and more narrowly than did the established leaders in Jerusalem.

Recently, sociologists have sought to develop a more inclusive typology of sects by defining them not over against a "church" but over against "the world"—that is, defining their relation to both the social structures of the society around them and the culture or "symbolic universe" of that society. Sects can thus be identified both in terms of the boundaries they maintain between their membership and the dominant society and in terms of their attitudes toward the world.[1] Both factors were of great importance in the ethos of the Qumran Essenes, as we saw in the previous chapter. The same is true of the early Christians, although the degree of separateness from "the world" and the degree of negativity expressed toward it varied considerably from one group of Christians to another.

Very soon after the death of Jesus, his followers took a major step toward sectarian identity by making baptism into a ritual of initiation. Unlike the initiatory rites of the mysteries so popular in the pagan world, but rather like the ceremony of entering the New Covenant practiced by the Essenes, baptism made the recipient part of a special community. We do not know who transformed it into a rite of entry into the new community, nor exactly where or when. Our earliest written documents from the Christian movement already presuppose that all Christians have received it, and that they also regularly share another unique ritual, the Lord's Supper.

Besides the special rituals that established membership in the movement of Jesus' followers, they probably separated from some other groups of Jews over the ritual observances that all Jews in some sense recognized—Sabbath observance, circumcision, kashruth, tithing, and so on. The Gospels contain a number of stories of controversies between Jesus and other Jews—most often Pharisees in the extant form of the stories—over such things. His disciples gather grain on the Sabbath; they do not wash ritually before eating; a person healed by Jesus carries his bed away, thus "working" on the Sabbath; healing itself may be forbidden work.

It is difficult to be sure of the extent to which such questions really separated the earliest Christians from other groups, for at least two reasons. First, there was apparently wide variation in practice among other Jews as well, and our sources do not permit much precision about what would have been expected of every ordinary Jew of no sectarian allegiance. Second, the Christian tradition is overlaid by concerns that developed very quickly as converts began to be made in the predominantly pagan cities. As we saw in the preceding chapter, some of the traditional practices had taken on new functions for Jews in that setting by helping to protect the Jewish communities from assimilation into the surrounding culture. Christian apostles disputed with one another whether proselytes from paganism must be circumcised and whether Christian groups ought to observe the Sabbath and the annual festivals, as we see most vividly in Paul's letter to the Galatians. These internal disputes, which would lead in the second century and even later to sectarian divisions within the Christian movement, doubtless affected the way in which the accounts of Jesus' controversies with opponents were recalled. So did the disputes between Christians and the new rabbinic academies that were taking shape after A.D. 70. Nevertheless, most evidence suggests that the followers of Jesus were lax in their observance of Sabbath and other rules—at least as viewed by Pharisees. The primary markers of group identity for them were something else.

A Jewish Sect

The controversies we have just mentioned do call attention again to the fact that the Christians began as a sect within the dominant Jewish culture of Palestine. Like any other Jewish sect, they addressed the question of correct behavior by asking what God has revealed as his will—what are his commandments?—and by inquiring about the form of obedience required of his people Israel. As it undertook to form the ethical sensibilities of its members, therefore, the sect could take for granted those fundamental ingredients of the Jewish world view that we discussed in chapter 3.

First, they believed that the God revealed to Israel of old is the only God. Like almost everyone else in the ancient world, most Jews also believed in a variety of other supernatural beings—angels, for example, and demons—and like all except those intellectuals of Epicurean persuasion, they knew that such *daimones* had power to affect human life. Jewish sources from Palestine in the Roman period picture this superhuman world in a rather more dualistic pattern than we find in literary sources from pagan authors. That is, there was a fundamental moral division in the divine world, on the one side God and his angels, on the other, Satan or the devil and his angels or "demons." The early Christians, insofar as our sources reveal, shared this dualist vision.

Second, Christians like other Jews believed that all morally significant knowledge was obtainable through an informed reading of the scriptures.

Third, they believed that human history has a shape and a meaning that are moral and theological. God presides over human affairs, acts in them, and judges them. Individuals, communities, and empires will be weighed at last by God's standard of perfect righteousness.

A Messianic Jewish Sect

The early followers of Jesus must be counted among the eschatological renewal movements that sprang up in the Land of Israel under Syrian and Roman rule. Of the others, the longest lived and now the best known was the sect that settled at Qumran. Perhaps the Pharisees, too, were such a movement, but from the surviving sources it is not clear whether eschatological beliefs were ever central for them. In addition, Josephus, in his *Antiquities,* tells of a number of prophets who appeared in Galilee, Samaria, and Judea in the period between Herod the Great's death and the outbreak of war in A.D. 66, who gathered followers and promised the fulfillment of Israel's classical hopes. The Roman governor routinely executed them and scattered their followers. Jesus' fate, like many aspects of his career, was familiar. To a casual observer, this sect stood out from the others in only one respect: it survived. It survived as it claimed Jesus survived, God having raised him from the dead and thus vindicated him as his Messiah.

The beginnings of the Christian movement belong, then, within the development of Jewish "apocalypticism," which is what modern scholars call the beliefs that probably motivated those renewal movements, because such beliefs are most vividly expressed in the kind of literature called "apocalypses." There are two elements in the earliest traditions preserved about Jesus which may justify placing his followers in this category. First, he is depicted as a prophet —sometimes as *the final* prophet—who called Israel to repentance and transformation with singular urgency. "The kingdom of God" was "at hand" (Mark 1:15). Second, those who continued his movement after his death now proclaimed that his career, and above all his crucifixion and resurrection, constituted the ultimate crisis for Israel. "Whoever is ashamed of me and of my words in this adulterous and sinful generation, of him will the Son of man [of Dan. 7:13] also be ashamed, when he comes in the glory of his Father with the holy angels" (Mark 8:38). Some Christians emphasized Jesus' prophetic teachings, some his death and resurrection, some both. All agreed in connecting the identity of the movement more intimately and exclusively with the identity of one person than was the case in any other Jewish sect we know about. In this last respect, the Christians were "messianic" in a special sense.

The Morals of an Apocalyptic Sect

Albert Schweitzer, who did more than anyone else to popularize the critical discovery that Jesus belonged to "Jewish apocalypticism," also called attention to the crisis which that discovery presented to any modern ethics that wanted to be based on Jesus' teachings. If Jesus shaped his career in expectation that very soon this world would end, then his moral teachings could have been only provisional and transitory—"an ethics of the interim."[2] This is not quite the right way of putting the problem, however, for the Qumran discoveries and further study of ancient apocalypses suggest that what the apocalyptic sect and its prophets typically foresaw was not simply the annihilation of the natural and human cosmos. The "end of the world" in that sense is a post-Christian fantasy. What attracted the apocalyptic sectary to his prophet was rather the promise that the world was soon to be transformed or replaced by a better world, in which righteousness would prevail. However dramatic the imagery of destruction sometimes found in apocalyptic texts, there was at least one line of continuity between this world and the new one: the faithful believers. The sect is to be the cadre of the new society that belongs to that new world. Consequently its ethic is, though provisional, nevertheless intended to be an infusion of the future light into the present darkness.

To be sure, the existence of the apocalyptic sect entails a radically negative judgment on this world. The sect is born out of a profound moral passion: the dominant society is in its eyes hopelessly corrupt.

> Do you think that these Galileans were worse sinners than all the other Galileans, because they suffered thus? I tell you, No; but unless you repent you will all likewise perish. Or those eighteen upon whom the tower in Siloam fell and killed them, do you think that they were worse offenders than all the others who dwelt in Jerusalem? I tell you, No; but unless you repent you will all likewise perish. (Luke 13:3–5)

Yet this condemning passion is not merely negative, for it implies a positive standard by which the present state of things is judged. Because by definition the sect is at odds with a society with which it shares fundamental perceptions and terms of discourse, the conflict of standards is a conflict between two ways of synthesizing the available norms from the classical tradition with the effects of recent history and present experience. It is not easy to say which comes first, alienation from the world or the vision of a righteous world, but certainly the two reinforce one another in the conversation of the sect.

Thus Schweitzer's statement of the issue he raised needs to be revised. The question whether the sectarian ethic could be adapted and eventually incorporated into a universal ethic is not so much a problem of the temporal limits of its horizons as the social boundaries of its definition of responsibility. Although the sect may have a vision of a righteous society, the existing "outside" society is so far from that vision that it may lie altogether outside the realm in which moral judgments count. The new member of the Qumran community, vowing to "love all the sons of light, each according to his lot in God's design," also pledged to "hate all the sons of darkness, each according to his guilt in God's vengeance" (1QS 1.9–11, Vermes). "He who is not with me is against me," said Jesus, "and he who does not gather with me scatters" (Matt. 12:30 = Luke 11:23). The explicit rules of a sect, as we saw in the case of Qumran, are likely to deal only with the internal cohesion and harmony of the sect itself and with the correlative value of maintaining its boundaries sharply against the rest of the world. Does a sectarian ethic then rightly deserve the name "ethics" at all? The moral logic of the position is more complex than first appears.

In one sense the sect has a very particularistic ethos: the rest of the world is on the road to damnation, and the sectary's moral obligation is first of all separation from that world. On the other hand, this judgment itself implies that the sect regards its own standards of judgment as the universally valid ones. It judges, it believes, with the judgment of (the one) God. There is here none of the live-and-let-live attitude which characterized urbane pagans of this era—and which was shared in practice by a vast number of Jews who had found a way to live comfortably in this pluralist world. The implicitly universal standards of the sect can be expressed either in withdrawal (Qumran), or in active proselytizing (early Christianity, perhaps some Pharisees), or in attempted reform by quiet example (the Pharisees, some early Christians?).

The form of the sect nevertheless circumscribes the members' perception of their moral responsibility. The universal scope that the sect attributes to its own values has the consequence of dividing the world into tightly separated circles: the great mass of humanity, who are hopelessly disobedient; the smaller circle of Israel, who have received the peculiar grace and obligation to fulfill the required righteousness; and the narrowest circle of the sect itself, who alone do uphold these standards.

The Socioecology of the Early Christian Sect[3]

The very early traditions about Jesus that have been preserved in the Synoptic Gospels depict him and his disciples wandering from village to village in the Galilee, preaching and performing miraculous healings and exorcisms. They have detached themselves from those ties of place and of family which, in a rural culture, ordinarily determine a person's identity:

> Foxes have holes, and birds of the air have nests; but the Son of man has nowhere to lay his head (Matt. 8:20 = Luke 9:58). Who are my mother and my brothers? . . . Whoever does the will of God is my brother, and sister, and mother (Mark 3:33–35). If any one comes to me and does not hate his own father and mother and wife and children and brothers and sisters, yes, and even his own life, he cannot be my disciple. (Luke 14:26; cf. Matt. 10:37)

They traverse a land where moral issues small and great cry out for solution, or so it seems to us. Yet they rarely address these issues directly. A young man appeals for help in getting his brother to divide fairly their father's estate; Jesus replies, "Man, who made me a judge or divider over you?" (Luke 12:14). Must one pay the taxes imposed by the Romans or, like Jesus' countryman Judas the "zealot," resist? Caesar's image is on the coin; pay him what is his—but pay to God [in whose image men and women are created?] what is *his* (Mark 12:13–17 and parallels). An arresting saying, but it hardly solves the problem. Jesus' parables take for granted the structures of an exploitative society: the distant landowner who sends his slaves to collect the rent from resentful sharecroppers; unemployed workers still standing idle in the town market at the end of the day; the exhausted slave coming in from plowing and ordered by his master to get cleaned up and fix his supper, no thanks expected; the beggar dying at the rich man's gate—and only in the last case is a moral judgment rendered.

Instead, many of the sayings of Jesus seem to demand an ascetic detachment from that whole world. Sending out his twelve specially chosen disciples,

> he charged them to take nothing for their journey except a staff; no bread, no bag, no money in their belts; but to wear sandals and not put on two tunics. And he said to them, "Where you enter a house, stay there until you leave the place. And if any place will not receive you and they refuse to hear you, when you leave, shake off the dust that is on your feet for a testimony against them." (Mark 6:8–11)

There were some circles in early Christianity who took such directives as a recipe for asceticism. Jesus and his immediate disciples provided a model for the ethos that discipleship required. In the *Gospel of Thomas,* for example, Jesus says: "Blessed are the solitary and elect, for you will find the Kingdom" (Saying 49).[4] The Greek word translated "solitary" is *monachos,* from which we get our word "monk." The urgent movement of Jesus and his messengers, preaching the "kingdom of God," here becomes characteristic of the life that wins salvation: "Jesus said, 'Become passers-by' " (Saying 42, Lambdin). The "solitary" does not detach himself from the settled world for the sake of an extraordinary mission, but because the world itself corrupts and kills: "Whoever has come to understand the world has found (only) a corpse, and whoever has found a corpse is superior to the world" (Saying 56, Lambdin).

The point of the saying found in the canonical Gospels and quoted above, however, is different. Notice that the radical separation of Jesus' messengers from the ordinary person's rootage in place, family, and livelihood requires for its fulfillment unqualified dependence upon the charity of strangers. The "asceticism" of the messengers is not the means of their salvation, so to speak, but the means for their mission. To be sure, it must be understood as prophetic symbol: a sign of the urgency of their message and of the exhaustive demand that the message makes on the hearer. It signals the same peremptoriness of the kingdom that is implied by such hyperbolic sayings of Jesus as, "If your hand trips you up, cut it off; it is better to enter life maimed than with two hands to go off to Gehenna" (Mark 9:43, my trans.). Nevertheless, the asceticism does not appear to be a model for life in the kingdom. It is rather, in an odd way, functional for the apostles' extraordinary mission. It makes demands on the hearers of a most extreme sort, in the sense that their reception of these messengers affects their standing before God (Mark 6:11; cf. the "Q" version in Matt. 10:13 and Luke

10:5–6). Yet they are not asked to imitate the itinerants, but only to listen to them and to support them—and the latter requires that they *not* abandon the world.

The availability of support for the mendicant preachers implies that they and the settled villagers who receive them share a common culture in which the message of the preachers makes some kind of sense, however radical its present form, and hospitality by a householder for such a wanderer is at least not unheard of. Something more is involved than the fabled hospitality of Middle Easterners, ancient and modern, for strangers accepted as guests. The messengers here fill a socially familiar role, a permutation of the classical role in Israel of the prophet.

If these "ascetic" sayings directed by Jesus to the Twelve really do give us an accurate picture of the activity or at least the ideals of his followers in the years immediately after his death, then we must revise the general picture of the sect drawn earlier in this chapter. There we emphasized the boundaries that the sect made between itself and its host culture; here we see a kind of symbiosis between that culture and the new movement. Moreover, these "wandering charismatics" are not represented as the entire sect or movement. Since the Gospels are ostensibly describing the situation in Jesus' earthly lifetime, they leave obscure what the relation was between the sect that formed after his death and these agents who must have been, in part, the means by which the sect drew new members from the Jewish villages. There are many hints in the Gospels and epistles and other early Christian literature that the relation was unclear even to the participants, and there were often conflicts over the role of the itinerant prophets. This much we can say with some confidence, however: the type of sayings we have sampled does not present an ethos that is demanded of the followers of Jesus as such. Rather, they outline the role of the itinerant prophet or apostle, who seems in the early years to have functioned at the borderline between the sect of Messiah Jesus and the larger society of the Palestinian villages. What were those villagers supposed to do if they believed the message of these prophets? In the body of tradition we have been looking at, that is left vague.

Yet this tradition readily lent itself to a variety of transformations as the sect adapted itself to different "ecologies." Thus once the Jesus sect had established itself in a number of places, the itinerants could narrow their horizons to the task of maintaining and correcting the faith of these Christian cells, and the expectations that they would be received and supported could be transferred from households selected out of the village in general to specifically

Christian households. Sometimes the local Christians saw them as nuisances or worse; hence the warnings against "false prophets and apostles" in the Gospels, the dispute between different factions reflected in the Second and Third Letters of John, and the rules for judging such people in the second-century church manual, the *Didache*. If the prophet says in a trance, "Give me money," for example, he is not to be heeded (*Didache* 11.22). At this stage of development, the mendicant preachers could exist outside the peasant society of common Jewish culture, for the existence of Christian cells in the cities around the Mediterranean soon gave them a subculture in which their role was also recognizable. Hence such apostles appear in congregations that Paul has founded, for example, in Galatia and in Corinth. Later a refugee from Judea, after the revolt against Rome, seems to have exercised such a role for a while in the towns of the province Asia; when the Romans exiled him to an island, he wrote to the Christian groups in those places a prophetic letter, "the Apocalypse of John."

One reason why the role of the wandering, begging prophet was understandable to new Christians in the Greek cities, even if they were not thoroughly schooled in the tradition of Israel's prophets, was the similarity between these prophets and the Cynics (see chapter 2). Even the physical appearance of the stereotyped Cynic is strikingly like that of the Twelve in Jesus' commission: both carry staffs, make do with a single garment, and depend on handouts. There is one difference—the begging bag or knapsack is a Cynic trademark (cf. the saying attributed to Crates, p. 26 above); the Twelve are forbidden to carry even that! (Mark 6:8). The transfer of this role from the Galilean and Judean villages into the Christian groups of the Greek cities thus introduced the possibility of assimilation between these two quite different cultural traditions. The eschatological challenge of the prophet to Israel could now be overlaid or replaced by the Cynic challenge to convention. The theonomous ethic implicit in the prophet's mission—to obey the will of God; to enter "the kingdom of God"—could be reinterpreted in terms of the *autarkeia* of the Cynic, his dramatic quest for the simplest life.

With or without the influence of the Cynic model, the tradition of an ascetic mission could become the ideal of an ascetic life as such. We have seen above in the examples from the *Gospel of Thomas* how separation from "the world," meaning everything that makes the normal society function—sex, family, commerce and money, the conventions of honor and shame, government—defines the Christian life. To "enter the kingdom of God," one must be "solitary"

—and thus find the kingdom inside oneself. Thus an eschatological ethos, adopted by prophets who called on people to confront an imminent transformation of life by God, becomes a way of life to be internalized. An ethos that had defined a sect becomes a way of salvation for individuals.

The adoption of asceticism as the central definition of the Christian ethos reached its most radical expression in movements beginning in the second century in two areas, eastern Syria and Egypt. The *Gospel of Thomas* and the *Acts of Thomas* probably were produced by Syrian ascetics or sympathizers; the one complete copy of the former that we have was found in Egypt, in a Coptic translation. The physical geography of those two areas is quite different, and consequently the Syrian and the Egyptian ascetics discovered different strategies for survival. In Egypt monks eventually joined together into wilderness communities. Thus was born the institution of the monastery. In Syria the "solitaries" existed on the margins of towns and villages and eventually re-created something like the symbiosis between villagers and prophet envisaged in the "apostolic" sayings of the Gospels, but in reverse. That is, now the monks settled in isolated places, and Christian villagers and even city dwellers came out to their hermitages for advice, inspiration, arbitration, healing, and, as time went on, many other services.

We have been exploring a few of the ways in which the rural ecology of parts of the early Christian movement may have affected the shape of the movement's ethos and ways it symbolized its ethical values. We have seen that sayings attributed to Jesus in the tradition could be taken as guides leading to one pattern of behavior in the early Palestine mission, to a quite different pattern in the Greek cities, and to still other patterns as those sayings were heard in other environments and at a later time in the Christian movement's development. In the ascetic movements we hear echoes of the tensions between town and country, between native societies and Rome, between citizens and resident aliens. We turn now to ways in which the church adapted to the institutions of the polis.

A Household Association in the Polis

The urgent prophesying of the Jesus movement quickly spilled over into the world outside Palestine. Just how this happened, or why, and whether other sects of Israel had similarly taken their message abroad (Matthew, at least, thought the Pharisees had so done: 23:15)—these are questions we cannot answer with precision. The author of the book of Acts, looking back from half a century or more, pictures the Greek-speaking converts of Jerusalem, "scattered because of the persecution that arose over Stephen," using their exile to spread the word of Jesus the Messiah to their fellow Jews (likewise Greek-speaking, of course) in places like Phoenicia and Cyprus and especially the great metropolis of Antioch-on-the-Orontes (Acts 11:19). Yet still earlier in the story, Acts tells about disciples in Damascus (9:1–2, 10–21). In each case, it is clear that the author thought of the Jesus group ("the Way," he calls it) as still a sect of Israel (see 24:5, 14; 28:22). The "ecology" of such a sect in the city, however, was manifestly different. Instead of a Jewish village, the traveling Christian would seek out some part of the Jewish association (Greek *synagōgē*) among the many such communities of resident aliens in the city. And these groups, the descendants of immigrants, were immersed in the pluralist, crowded, public society of the city to an extent unimaginable in a Palestinian village. It was in Antioch, Acts tells us, that some of the exiled prophets first "spoke to the Greeks also" (11:20). Certainly the wandering preachers would bring with them to the city that "sectarian" ethos which characterized the Christian movement in the villages of Israel—but it is equally certain that that ethos would have to be transformed in the new environment.

In the Synagogue

It is altogether plausible to imagine the Christian prophets bringing their challenge to the Jewish community in each city as they had done before in Jerusalem or in the villages. To be sure, there is not very much early evidence to support this later picture in Acts, but there is some. Thus it is commonly acknowledged that the Roman historian Suetonius' report, that the emperor Claudius ordered the Jews out of Rome because of continuing "disturbances instigated by Chrestus" (*Life of Claudius* 25.4), implies that Christian preachers had produced a schism in the Jewish community in Rome itself. That report fits in with the note in Acts 18:2. The Gospel of John presupposes Christian groups who see themselves entirely within the orbit of Jewish communities, but nevertheless in a Greek-speaking town or towns somewhere. Those Jewish communities, and especially their officers, had become very hostile to the sect that made such blasphemous claims for Jesus ("equal to God"), and the leaders of the Christian community despised secret believers in Jesus who wanted to remain in the Jewish community. Probably when the Fourth Gospel was written, this time of intense controversy was past, and the separation complete. In any case by the time the Letters of John were written, in the same circles, the sect seems no longer to have been interested in contacts with "the Jews." There may have been many more instances of Christian proselytizing and the formation of cells of followers of Jesus the Messiah within urban Jewish communities than our sources reveal. One ancient version of the daily synagogue prayer ("The Eighteen Benedictions") includes a clause that curses not only "sectaries" *(minim)* as other versions do, but specifically "Nazoreans," a name often used of the Christians in early sources. However, the date, earliest form, and use of this *Birkat ha-minim* ("blessing of the sectaries") are all matters of scholarly debate.[5]

On the whole, it is likely that the Christians made their appearance in the Greek cities as a sect within the Jewish communities. As this sect developed its own life in the urban environment, it doubtless absorbed many of the ways of thinking and took as its own many of the ways of adapting to the pluralist culture around it that generations of other Jews had learned. Nevertheless, in many places—including all of the congregations founded by Paul and his associates, which are the ones we know best—they very early became independent in identity and organization. The book of Acts itself shows us the common institution which made that independence possible, and the letters of the New Testament as well as archaeology confirm the fact: it was the private household.

The Household

The early chapters of Acts depict the Jerusalem Christians as very observant Jews, centering many of their activities in the Temple. However, several details mentioned in the stories reveal that the distinctive life of the Christian groups went on in private homes (e.g., Acts 2:46; 12:12). This was even more clearly the case in the cities of the Diaspora. Thus in Corinth Paul moves in first with the tentmakers Aquila and Priscilla, then later with one Titius Justus, whose "house was next door to the synagogue" (Acts 18:2–3, 7). It was not a matter only of traveling missionaries lodging in such homes, moreover. In several places in his letters Paul sends greetings to or from the "assembly" or "meeting" *(ekklēsia)* in someone's house. "The church" (as we usually translate *ekklēsia*) in each city thus typically consisted of a number of small cells meeting in various private houses. Where the Christians were lucky enough to find a convert or sympathizer who could afford a more spacious house, all the cells in a city might come together on occasion for worship and instruction (1 Cor. 14:23; Rom. 16:23). In time the house might be given, sold, or bequeathed to the Christian community that met there. The earliest Christian building identified by archaeologists, a third-century house in the Roman garrison town Dura Europos, is an example, remodeled for exclusive use by the sect not long before the town was destroyed. This was a pattern often followed by cults new to a city; the Mithraeum of Dura had a similar history, though longer and more elaborate. So did the Dura synagogue and several other ancient synagogues discovered in recent years.

The private house offered obvious advantages to a sect being transplanted to a city. It provided a modicum of privacy in a setting where most life is public, and it was a stable place where the group could meet and hold their own special rituals—not so isolated, however, that curious neighbors would not have an idea what was going on, or that uninitiated folk could not peek in and be offended if "charismatics" were out of control (1 Cor. 14:23). The house-holder became in effect the patron of the group, offering not only the place and probably some financial support but also protection. Jason, for example, posts bond to assure the good behavior of his guests in Thessalonica (Acts 17:9). Here we see at work a variation on an arrangement that was ubiquitous in the society of the Greek as well as the Latin cities: patron and clients, the ties of mutual advantage that bound socially and economically superior folk to an assortment of their inferiors. What did the patron get in return? Honor, chiefly, a most precious commodity in ancient society, as we have seen. Hence the inscriptions that survive from ancient club-rooms recording votes to erect a statue of the club's benefactor, or award him a golden wreath, or the perpetual right of the "first seat" at the club's banquets—there is an example of such a vote of wreath and *proedria* by a synagogue in Phocae to a generous pagan.[6] Paul has to remind the Christians in Corinth to give proper deference to patrons like Stephanas. But there are other notions of honor and other kinds of leaders in the Christian groups, and Paul mentions "all the fellow workers and laborers" alongside Stephanas (1 Cor. 16:15f.).

The fact that Christian groups were often grafted onto house-holds affected the way they grew. Acts speaks often of some-one being converted with all his or her household. That did not always happen; the slave Onesimus was converted only after he ran away from his Christian master Philemon. There were Christians who had pagan spouses (1 Cor. 7:12–16; 1 Peter 3:1f.) as well as slaves with pagan masters (1 Peter 2:18–20; Hippolytus, *Apostolic Tradition* 15, Botte). In any case, the household had its own network of natural connections, within and without: kinship, friendship among social equals of its members, patron-client connections with others up and down the social scale, affiliations of trade or craft. Along such lines could move news about the new faith, curiosity, and attraction to it.

The obverse side of such useful connections was that the Christian group in Stephanas' or Gaius' household was engaged in the larger society of the polis in innumerable ways. Sometimes such engagement produced conflicts that did not arise or at least were not so sharp for the Jesus-followers in Jewish villages. Networks of friendship would entail invitations to dinner. Meat might be served; not merely not kosher, but bought in the public markets and therefore probably supplied by one or another of the city's temples, the remains of sacrifices to some god. Most butchers were priests in antiquity, and vice versa. Can Christians eat it? Would eating be idolatry? A sharp division at Corinth led some of the leaders to write to Paul (1 Cor. 8–10). The issue was still alive in the province Asia at the end of the century; the prophet John took it very seriously and would not have liked Paul's complicated solution (Rev. 2:14, 20). Issues like this had of course confronted the Jewish communities in the pagan cities for generations, and the urban Jews had worked out various ways of participating in necessary ways in the city's life while protecting the identity and integrity of their faith and their community. Even within these established Jewish communities there were disagreements as well as differences from one city to another.

Such eschatological enthusiasm as that which motivated the new Jesus-followers, however, is something we rarely hear of in Jewish writings from the Greek cities. It seems to have produced a disposition among the apostles to the cities to modify, ignore, or discard the ordinary Jewish rules for proselytes, and that required rethinking the whole question of the boundaries between "God's people" and "the world." The most vehement arguments swirled around Paul and his associates, but they were surely not the only ones to raise these issues.

The structure of the household itself and the ways people thought about the household contained the potential for moral conflict among the Christians in numerous ways. Aristotle, as we saw in chapter 1, took the household as a paradigm of the political order. Like the polis itself, it is made up of people of different rank. Some are fit to rule (free males, owners, fathers), others to serve (women, children, slaves). Equity in transactions between such roles is not equality, but proper proportion. Aristotle thus stated systematically and succinctly what was common belief (at least among those who ruled, who also wrote the books) in his time. The same sentiments were repeated and expanded by philosophers after him, and in Roman times they were a commonplace to be found in handbooks of philosophy. Upset the order of the home, people believed, and the whole society was in trouble. Yet when converts were initiated into the Christian group they might hear the strange proclamation that with their clothing they had "stripped off the old human" who was divided in those ways, "putting on" in his place" the "new human, Christ," in whom "there is no slave nor free, no Jew nor Greek, no male and female" (Col. 3:9–11; Eph. 4:22–24; Gal. 3:27f.). What could that mean? Women did play a very large part in the mission and patronage and leadership of the Pauline groups, and that may well have been the case also in the other urban missions about which we know much less. In Rome, for example, there was a certain Junia who, with Andronicus (her husband?), was "foremost among the apostles" (Rom. 16:7). Must such women after all remain "submissive"? If Philemon granted Paul's request and received his runaway slave back, "no longer as a slave but more than a slave, a beloved brother—especially to me, but still more to you: in the flesh as well as in the Lord" (Philemon 26, my trans.), what would Onesimus' status now be? That these were real and troubling questions is clear from the fact that in the second generation leaders were writing letters in the names of Paul and Peter and others emphasizing anew the old Aristotelian rules: "Wives, be subject to your husbands, as is fitting in the Lord. . . . Slaves, obey in everything those who are your earthly masters" (Col. 3:18–4:1; Eph. 5:22–6:9; 1 Peter 2:18–3:7).

Cultic Association

Obviously the Christian assembly was not simply identical with the household onto which it was grafted. With its regular meetings, its strong sense of identity, its special meals, it had the character of a voluntary association, a club. Clubs were very popular in the Greek and Roman cities—with everyone except the Roman authorities, who were chary of private meetings, where conspiracies might be hatched. Mainly the clubs existed for the sake of conviviality, especially for people of like interests or occupations. Poorer people formed societies to provide for their funerals. Imperial laws against associations make an exception for such burial-insurance societies, as well as for old, established religious associations. The Christian groups were neither old nor established, and their private meetings and odd rituals were likely to lead to suspicions about their morality and their political intentions.

The Christian groups were evidently a special kind of club; one was admitted, after all, only by a kind of *initiation.* To be sure, almost every contemporary club was religious in some sense: dedicated to a god or gods, whose festival days would be celebrated by proper ceremonial. And there were special associations of devotees to the great gods of the initiatory mysteries—Demeter and Persephone, Isis and Sarapis, Dionysus and the rest. Yet being initiated into one of these cults did not ordinarily entail becoming part of an association. Such cultic associations were either professional societies of priests and other functionaries employed by the cults, or they were honorary societies of persons especially devoted to the gods, who would thus participate in the major public spectacles of the cults—festivals, processions, theatrical performances, and so on—or provide for the upkeep of the temples and their personnel. Christian initiation, which made of the baptized "children of God" and brothers and sisters of one another, was different.

The Christian associations were different in another respect, particularly important for our present subject. Religious cults in antiquity had little directly to do with ethics. Sometimes the rules posted for participation in a cult reflect common moral values, and they would thus tend to reinforce them: "Let those who enter this house, men and women, free and slaves, swear by all the gods that they are aware of no trickery exercised against man or woman, nor know nor carry out any evil spell or wicked enchantment against persons, or love-charm or abortifacient, or contraceptive, or any other means of infanticide, that they have neither made these themselves nor advised or assisted another so to do, that they have cheated no one."[7] Yet there is little evidence that cults undertook to establish or reform moral rules or to instruct their adherents in ethical principles or rules for behavior. Such instruction belonged rather, as we saw in chapter 2, to the schools of philosophy and rhetoric, and to the public discourse by philosophers and orators. The Christian groups did concern themselves with the behavior of their members, from the beginning; in this respect, it has been suggested, they may have looked more like a school than a cult.

Christian Schools

The earliest piece of Christian literature we possess is a moral exhortation sent by letter from Paul to the recent converts he had left in Thessalonica.[8] As so often in the hortatory literature of antiquity, pagan, Jewish, or Christian, much of the letter consists in reminders, emphasizing things that the readers already know. Some of these things they know because they experienced them: Paul's arrival among them, their own conversion, some subsequent troubles, and the visit of Timothy. Others they know because everyone of good sense knew them: for instance, it was good for people like them to live a quiet life, minding their own business. In addition, however, Paul and his fellow writers remind the Thessalonian Christians, "We gave you certain precepts through the Lord Jesus" (1 Thess. 4:2, my trans.), of which they proceed to give examples. It looks, then, as if the process of conversion already entailed (the letter was written not much more than twenty years after Jesus' crucifixion) some explicit instruction. And that instruction included not only the special beliefs of the Christian sect but also "how you ought to behave [lit., "to walk"] and to please God" (1 Thess. 4:1). Furthermore, the very same rule that Paul cites here, which has to do with marriage (v. 4), he paraphrases and expounds in a letter addressed to another congregation (1 Cor. 7:2).[9] At least within the circle of Paul and his associates, then, there was some consistency in such instruction from one place to another. So Paul could praise the Corinthian group for sticking with "the traditions" he "delivered" to them (1 Cor. 11:2), although other aspects of their behavior he found not praiseworthy (1 Cor. 11:17), and in fact not in accord with other traditions he had likewise passed on to them (v. 23).

The "precepts" employed by the Pauline leaders in their instruction and admonitions included, besides such rules as the one quoted in 1 Thessalonians 4:4, sayings of Jesus used in the same way. Thus when confronted with a question about divorce, Paul says, "I direct —rather, not I but the Lord—that a woman not separate from her husband . . . and a man not divorce his wife" (1 Cor. 7:10, my trans.). The verb translated "direct" (*parangellein*) is cognate with the noun translated "precept" (*parangelia*) in 1 Thessalonians 4:2. We know the precept about divorce also from the Synoptic Gospels (Mark 10:2–9; Matt. 19:9; Matt. 5:31f. = Luke 16:18). Small variations in the rule from one place to another are evidence that the various Christian groups undertook to put it into practice, but found that it required interpretation and adjustment. (Notice that Paul also qualified the application in 1 Cor 7:11.) Thus there is good reason to suppose that sayings of Jesus that lent themselves to application as rules were so used in many different circles of the early Christian movement. Indeed, that is doubtless one reason why sayings of Jesus were collected and eventually written down. We know of at least two such early collections: one compiled before the last quarter of the first century and used by both Matthew and Luke, the other produced probably some time in the second century and now known as the *Gospel of Thomas*. Other bits and pieces have survived on papyrus, and early Christian authors often quote sayings otherwise unknown. These facts suggest that there may have been many such collections, whether oral or written.[10] The existence of these collections is itself evidence for ethical instruction in the Christian communities.

From the second century we have clearer evidence for the regular instruction of converts. Sometime in the middle of the century, for example, a kind of manual for church officers was compiled, using older sources, and presented under the title *The Teaching* [*didachē*] *of the Twelve Apostles*. Before baptizing, it directs, "Give public instruction on all these points [i.e., the precepts of the preceding chapters]" (7.1).[11] Scholars think that substantial parts of the *Didache*'s regulations were already used, perhaps in Syria, in the first century, but it is not certain how early they included formal prebaptismal instruction. By the end of the second century, in Rome, such instruction had become very elaborate. We know this from a document called *The Apostolic Tradition,* produced early in the third century by a certain Hippolytus. Indignant when he was passed over for the office of pope, Hippolytus wrote *The Apostolic Tradition* to show the high standard from which he thought the church was now declining. Most scholars think that, while he was hardly an objective reporter, the *Tradition* really does represent the practice or at least the ideal of orthodox Roman Christians in the last part of the previous century. The *Apostolic Tradition* orders that "those who present themselves for the first time to hear the Word are to be brought before the teachers" for examination (15, ed. Botte, my trans.). After initial screening, they are ordinarily to be instructed for three years before being admitted to baptism (17), and during that "catechumenate" (from the Greek word for "a person being instructed") their behavior is carefully monitored.

There is evidence in the early literature not only for ethical and other instruction of converts but also for "scholarly" activity that impinges on the development of Christian ethics. That is, there are signs that many of the leaders of the new movement were acquainted with the explicit moral traditions and the methods of their cultivation which prevailed in their cultural environment. For example, in the collection of sayings of Jesus used by the Gospel writers "Matthew" and "Luke," commonly called "Q," many characteristics of the scribal wisdom tradition appear. This is apparent in many of the forms of the individual sayings—parables, aphorisms, proverbs, and so on—and also in such things as the use of examples out of Israel's history and scripture—Noah, Jonah, Solomon, David. Of course, at least some of these sayings were doubtless really spoken by Jesus, and he may have seen himself as belonging to the wisdom tradition. The ancients did not necessarily make the same sharp distinctions between "wisdom" and "prophecy" that scholars now do. In any case, some of Jesus' followers certainly saw in him a sage in the familiar pattern, and they handed on his sayings in forms appropriate to that image. The fact that a number of these sayings occur in more than one version in the Gospels and other early Christian literature implies further that the leaders of the new Christian movement did not merely memorize and repeat them, but also worked on them, revising and adapting them to the changing circumstances of the sect. Such interpretations were, no doubt, often made extemporaneously, but sometimes there are signs of more deliberate, "scholarly" exposition: the three versions of the "Parable of the Great Supper" in the Gospels of Luke and Matthew, and in the *Gospel of Thomas,* for instance. Another example, outside the "Q" collection, is the interpretation of the Parable of the Sower, applying it to the experience of Jesus' followers after they had become an actively proselytizing sect (Mark 4:13–20 and parallels).

Such cultivation and (re)interpretation of sages' words was part of the classic vocation of the "scribe," who, according to Ben Sira, "will seek out the wisdom of all the ancients, and will be concerned with prophecies; he will preserve the discourse of notable men and penetrate the subtleties of parables" (Sirach 39.1f.). The authors of the Gospels continued this interpretative activity; it is especially evident in Matthew. For good reason commentators have thought the simile of the ideal scribe in Matt. 13:52 might be an appropriate self-portrait of the author himself: "Every scribe who has been trained for the kingdom of heaven is like a householder who brings out of his treasure what is new and what is old."

Evidence for appropriation by the early Christians of learned traditions of moral instruction and advice abounds not only in the Gospels but in other kinds of early Christian literature as well. Paul's letters sometimes contain such subtle expositions of biblical texts that one may wonder how many of the converted pagans in his congregations really followed the argument. For example, 1 Corinthians 10:1–13 is an elaborate and most carefully constructed midrash on the text, "And the people sat down to eat and drink, and rose up to play" (Ex. 32:6). To appreciate its artistry and its logic, the reader needs a detailed knowledge of the biblical story of Israel's sojourn in the wilderness after the exodus, especially certain events recorded in Numbers, and also an awareness of the wide range of ways the verb translated "to play" is used in scripture. The Letter of James, a more general example of hortatory literature, is filled with parallels to both Jewish and pagan traditions of moral instruction. One thread that holds together its rather miscellaneous admonitions is a series of allusions to Leviticus 19—a chapter that was used for a similar purpose not only in later rabbinic traditions but also in some Greek Jewish moral literature roughly contemporary with James.[12] Evidently the early Christian teachers sometimes took over and "recycled" Jewish works of moral instruction or exhortation. The *Testaments of the Twelve Patriarchs* is another example of such adaptation. In its extant form, it is a Christian work of uncertain date, but it clearly has incorporated a great quantity of Jewish moralizing interpretation of the biblical stories of the Patriarchs.

It was not only Jewish scholarship that affected early Christian ethical thinking, however. The works just cited, Paul, James, and the *Testaments of the Twelve Patriarchs,* all exhibit acquaintance with the kinds of issues that were discussed in Greek rhetorical and philosophical schools and with some of the patterns of teaching that those schools employed. In varying degrees, the same is true of much early Christian literature. Acquaintance with rhetorical conventions is more obvious in such relatively polished compositions as the Letter to the Hebrews, or even 1 Peter. Later authors strive more transparently to exhibit their education. Some of the apologists of the second and third centuries, like the Latin writer Minucius Felix, have obviously had literary training, and the great Alexandrian scholars Clement and Origen write as self-confident intellectuals. In the case of the first-century writers, such as Paul, it is hard to be sure whether the similarities we discover between their works and the traditions of the schools are the result of their having had a formal higher education, or whether such knowledge represents the penetration of popular culture by the elite traditions. We do know that people by the thousands sometimes turned out to hear a famous orator, and very often what they heard was a discourse on an ethical topic (look, for example, at the subjects addressed by Dio Chrysostom's orations, conveniently collected in the Loeb Classical Library). No one has yet tried to measure the influence of rhetoric on the taste and moral values of the uneducated residents of the Greco-Roman city, but at least it was a medium by which they were exposed to some of the commonplaces of those "great traditions" we considered in chapter 2. Moreover, the intertwining of Greek and Roman traditions with distinctively Jewish interpretive traditions, which we have seen in many of our early Christian documents, makes it very likely that Christian leaders may have received some of these traditions already woven together by Jewish moralists of the Diaspora cities. Philo was certainly not the only Jewish intellectual who labored at that task.

By the second century, the kind of scholastic activity that may be deduced from the earlier evidence was becoming institutionalized —for example, the instruction of new converts. In Rome we hear of a number of individuals who give regular instruction to circles of inquirers, very much in the pattern of a Musonius Rufus or an Epictetus, and probably in conscious imitation of such philosophers. That certainly is the case with Justin and in turn with his former pupil Tatian, despite the latter's studied disdain for Greek values. Another famous example was the mystical, Platonist Christian Valentinus, whose "gnostic" speculations, however, soon led mainstream church leaders to attack him as a heretic. The pattern of individual schools did not make it easy to define or to enforce an orthodoxy. Eventually bishops would establish their own schools.

The emergence of Christian scholarship was an important means by which the countercultural sect of the crucified Messiah's followers would eventually assimilate to the new society that would take shape in late antiquity. From the beginning, it seems, there were some leaders in the sect who were able, consciously or unconsciously, to connect the Christian movement's moral and religious reflections with the Great Traditions, both Jewish and Gentile. The Greek and Roman heritage would naturally become more dominant with the passage of time, but the Jewish was so integral to the earliest forms of the sect that it could not be disowned altogether. Even at times when the church leaders expressed most hostility toward the Jews, inherited forms of Jewish scriptural interpretation continued to be influential, and some Christian scholars—Origen, Jerome, Aphrahat, for example—continued to learn from and argue with Jewish teachers. By that time, however, the fundamental shape of Christian moral discourse had been set, and it was quite different from that which was being formed in the same era in the rabbinic academies (on the latter, see the end of chapter 3).

Church

Something new was emerging in the private homes where believers in "Jesus the Christ" gathered, in the townwide gatherings for the Lord's Supper that a wealthier householder sometimes made possible, in the small circles of catechumens taking instruction from a Christian "philosopher." The new thing was what we call "the church," but it is not easy to define it or to specify its newness. It was all the old things that observers in the first century might have seen in it: a Jewish sect, a club meeting in a household, an initiatory cult, a school. Yet it was more than the sum of those things, and different from the mere synthesis of their contradictory tendencies.

It is not only our ignorance and distant angle of vision that make defining the church problematical; the early Christians themselves had a great deal of trouble deciding just what their movement was and what it ought to become. From the earliest times there were differences not only of opinion but of the very shape of the movement, and the New Testament as well as the later Christian documents are filled with evidence of collisions between different groups and different ways of construing what Christianity was. Those conflicts themselves, however, betray one of the peculiarities of the church among other ancient organizations and movements: some internal drive toward unity and even uniformity of belief and behavior. The drive was almost always frustrated; when uniformity was obtained, it was usually at the cost of exclusion or schism or suppression. Nevertheless, the drive persisted.

This odd, stubborn conviction that the Christian movement was, or ought to be, one and the same in all places was almost certainly derived somehow from its origin as a Jewish messianic sect. Israel was one as its God was one, and the Diaspora experience only heightened the significance of both beliefs. The Jesus sect, however, convinced that the prophet crucified in Jerusalem was the Messiah of God and that his resurrection inaugurated the beginning of the new age of God's reign, launched a last-chance mission to let everyone know. For some of these missionaries, "everyone" included not just Jews wherever they might live, but Gentiles too, for the new age would be a new beginning for humankind. Their initiation ceremony was filled with allusions to the stories of creation, paradise, and fall; they sometimes called Christ "the new human" or "the last Adam." Thus the images of unity which had served and shaped Israel were now transmuted to serve a movement whose boundaries crossed the line between Jew and Gentile, which wanted to be, in the moments when its imagination was most audacious, not only the one people of God but also the new humanity.

The Christian symbols of unity are not our immediate subject; we are interested in the way these beliefs were embodied in the social forms of the church and in their expectations about the behavior of members. Early on we do find leaders asserting the desired unity as a warrant for behavior. Paul, or perhaps a more "conservative" disciple editing his letter, could insist on women being quiet in meetings, "as in all the assemblies [*ekklēsiai*] of the saints" (1 Cor. 14:33). Earlier in the same letter Paul insists of female prophets not that they should keep quiet, but only that they should keep their hair covered. It was unthinkable for them to have short or uncovered hair, as for men in the same circumstance to have long hair. If anyone was unpersuaded by his argument (few modern readers have even understood it!), he adds: "We have no such custom, nor do the assemblies [*ekklēsiai*] of God" (1 Cor. 11:16, my trans.).

The very fact that people like Paul, his associates, and sometimes his opponents trekked from city to city revisiting the Christian communities, and that when they could not do that they sent letters instructing and admonishing them about how they ought to live, also bears witness to the importance of the peculiar Christian itch for unity. Several other kinds of letters give evidence of the same tendency. Even within the New Testament there are letters that were intended as "encyclicals," to be circulated to several places. First Peter is addressed to "the exiles of the Dispersion in Pontus, Galatia, Cappadocia, Asia, and Bithynia"—here the adoption of Jewish language and the transmutation of the immigrant experience are manifest, as they are also, more universally and more metaphorically, in the address of the Letter of James. The Apocalypse of John is a letter addressed to "the seven *ekklēsiai* that are in [the Roman province] Asia" (Rev. 1:4). Sometime earlier a disciple of Paul had written a letter probably circulated to some of the same churches; we know it as "the Letter to the Ephesians." The Letter to the Hebrews is a "hortatory speech" (*logos parakleseōs,* 13:22) dispatched as a letter. Toward the end of the first century the church in Rome wrote a long letter (called *1 Clement*) to Christians in Corinth, containing both general moral exhortation and specific admonition about the governance of the church. The letter cites Paul's letters as precedent for this intervention in the affairs of another community. These examples could be multiplied.

The sense of extralocal identity of the "assemblies" or people of God had both immediate and long-term consequences for the ethos of Christianity. In the near term it generated a pressure toward imposing or trying to impose conformity that was not usual either in Greco-Roman cults or, insofar as we can tell from the records, in Diaspora Judaism. On the other hand, it produced in many of the new Christians a sense of belonging to an association, indeed a brotherhood, that extended far beyond the limits of any other clubs of the time we know about, except perhaps the synagogues themselves. This sense became real experience in numerous small and practical ways. A traveler to a distant city, armed with a letter of recommendation from a recognized leader (like Paul's for Phoebe, Rom. 16:1f.), could find there not merely friends but "brothers and sisters," ready to offer hospitality. These brothers and sisters might even be prepared to offer support and help in case of trouble, such as conflict with authorities. The pagan satirist Lucian gleefully describes all that the Christians did for an itinerant prophet, one Peregrinus Proteus, as examples of what Lucian took to be their gullibility. When Peregrinus was imprisoned, not only did Christians in the place make extraordinary efforts to help him, but "people came even from the cities in Asia, sent by the Christians at their common expense, to succour and defend and encourage the hero." Lucian had learned that they did such things because "their first lawgiver persuaded them that they are all brothers of one another after they have transgressed once for all by denying the Greek gods and by worshipping that crucified sophist himself and living under his laws" (*The Passing of Peregrinus* 13).[13]

In the long term, the Christian drive toward unity and universality would give to the church an almost imperial structure. Again, this was not the result of a plan or coherent doctrine or any single factor, but the result of many developments, some symbolic, some practical. The emergence of a single "overseer" (*episkopos,* hence "bishop") in each city, replacing the older, looser organization, like that of Jewish communities, with councils of elders, coincided in the second century with a rising concern to control divisive movements of doctrine and practice. Ignatius the bishop of Antioch, even as he was being transported to Rome for trial and, as he expected and desired, death, conducted a campaign by letter and in person, through the cities of Asia, for recognition in every place of the authority of a single bishop. The unity of the church in each city (and its dependent villages) must be found in a single office, the bishop, and moreover the unity of the universal church must lie in the solidarity of all those local bishops. The great ecumenical councils of the subsequent centuries of doctrinal controversy embodied the further development of Ignatius' vision, however much they also exhibited the difficulty of bringing it about.

The church as empire was also suggested by its own experience of opposition to the provincial governing structures of Rome. We see this most clearly in two kinds of early Christian literature, the apocalypses and the martyrologies. In both, ancient images of cosmic struggles between the dragon of chaos and a God of order reappear to depict a war of God's agents and people against Rome. The mythic imagery itself made both sides seem more monolithic than they were in fact. Ironically, our tendency to imagine that the

Roman empire under such emperors as Domitian was a totalitarian government, like twentieth-century police states, is made possible precisely by these apocalyptic images. The real difficulties experienced by the Christians were much more local, occasional, and irregular. By the time, in the middle of the third century, when the emperor came to perceive Christianity as a real threat to public order and undertook to break its organization, he lacked effective means for accomplishing that. The more effective emperors did undertake to reform provincial government in order to establish more centralized and more uniform control; by a further irony, a development in some ways parallel was taking place among the bishops. By the time Constantine decided to join the Christians, the two empire-wide organizations, the Christian church and the Roman state, stood side by side. Eusebius' unabashed panegyric on Constantine and the early Byzantine mosaics of Christ as *pantokratōr*, emperor of the universe, are two witnesses to the Christian triumphalism that followed the wedding of the two empires. Augustine's *City of God* mutes that triumphalism to some extent and dwells on the paradox of the two communities living together on earth.

5

The Grammar
of Early Christian Morals

In the previous chapter we saw that the settings and shapes of various circles of the early Christian movement, changing over time as the movement developed, affected the ways the Christians construed their moral tasks. Not only the concrete possibilities of what they could do, but also their very perception of what was to be done depended to some extent on the places where they found themselves in the diverse society of the Roman empire. The range of obligations and possibilities was not the same, for example, for a Judean villager responding to an itinerant prophet of Messiah Jesus as it would be for the dependent of a well-to-do householder in Corinth whose house had become the location of a Christian "meeting."

Still, the correspondence between social structures and the patterns of perceived moral obligation is by no means exact; much less is it a one-way street. Whatever there was in the world of second-century Syrian Christians that made them hear the directives of Jesus to his apostles as prescriptions for the Christian life-warfare against the world, it was the directives themselves, heard that way, which they tried with all their might to put into practice. The forms of one's life shape one's beliefs, but the beliefs have a force of their own, and power to shape the forms of life.

In this final chapter we will be concerned not so much with the world around the early Christian groups as with the world within. What was the shape of the life they strove to live? What were its boundaries and what was its center? What and who resided beyond the boundaries, and how ought the Christian to regard and interact with that "outside" world? What is the inner logic of Christian moral perceptions and moral sensibilities?

In keeping with the general plan of this inquiry, we shall undertake to observe—that is, to reconstruct from some of the surviving sources—the process by which the moral intuitions of people within the Christian movement were formed. What we are after is not merely the logic of their ideas but the grammar of their sensibilities and their behavior, which of course includes the force of ideas.

As in the earlier chapters on the moral traditions of their "outside" world, the materials we have to work with are texts, fragments of the ethical discourse that helped to form the character of the early Christians. As before, too, we can only treat a few representative samples of the texts that survive. And "representative" is subject to correction, for limits of space prompt concentration here on texts that were later deemed central in the emerging "catholic" consensus. Through even these texts we hear quite a few dissonant voices, but not so clearly as we might if we had room to consider the literature, mostly later than what we are examining, that survives from those movements which came to be regarded as "heretical" or schismatic. We shall take up our samples in roughly chronological order, beginning with the earliest extant Christian writing.

Most studies of these texts concentrate on their theological ideas, but our present inquiry requires a different focus. In fact, we will see in each case that the writers of the texts were centrally concerned to affect the behavior, not just the thinking, of their audiences. We will be looking for characteristic ways in which they tried to affect behavior, and the reasons the methods of moral guidance they chose would have seemed appropriate and effective in their situations.

A Letter of Moral Admonition: 1 Thessalonians

The earliest complete Christian writing that we have is a letter of moral exhortation, which the Greeks called *parainesis* (a word now often taken into English as "parenesis").[1] Written by the apostle Paul, with his colleagues Silvanus and Timothy, to the Christian groups he had only recently established in Thessalonica, it is an ideal place to begin our detective work. Not only does this letter remind the recent converts of some of the basic beliefs, rules, and moral expectations that they learned earlier, it also exhibits some of the strategies used by the founders to encourage the kind of life they think appropriate.

The "sectarian" form of the early Christian movement, which we discussed in the previous chapter, is immediately apparent in 1 Thessalonians. The letter looks back on a process that began with the "turning" or "conversion" of the addressees "from idols, to serve a living and true God" (1:9). That "turning" led to a separation from relatives and neighbors, even hostility from those who were formerly closest to the converts. Paul acknowledges that estrangement and uses it to stress the solidarity that the converts have with Christians elsewhere (2:14) and with Jesus himself. Indeed, very much of what is said in this letter works to suggest that the ties of kinship and friendship severed by conversion are replaced by even deeper connections with the new family of God in Christ. In surprisingly emotion-loaded language Paul recalls his own connections with the converts and his feelings about them. He even reflects the typical convert's experience of being "orphaned" in the word he chooses to speak of his pain at being separated from them (2:17). Thus the letter itself becomes part of a process of resocialization which undertakes to substitute a new identity, new social relations, and a new set of values for those which each person had absorbed in growing up.

No conversion, however, is ever total. The process of resocialization cannot simply obliterate the ways of thinking, feeling, and valuing that were part of the person before the change began. The degree of change will vary from one person to the next, and not all aspects of anyone's personality will be equally affected by conversion. Further, as we saw in chapter 4, the early Christian movement itself was not always and everywhere identical; it adapted continually to different environments. The Christian groups in Thessalonica already represent that decisive second stage of the movement's development: no longer a Jewish environment, but predominantly Gentile; no longer a village culture but that of a Greek city. All through Paul's letter there are elements, including even its general form, which are typical of pagan moral rhetoric. Yet there are also elements which are distinctively Jewish, which reflect the lessons learned by generations of Jews concerned to maintain their integrity as God's special people in pagan cities. The two are, moreover, often so intertwined that they cannot be easily separated. Is there in the mix something novel, something distinctively Christian?

Like any parenetic letter, 1 Thessalonians is filled with reminders of what the recipients already know. "As you know" is a refrain (e.g., 1:5; 2:2, 5, 11; 3:4); further, they are reminded of specific "precepts" which the founders gave them (4:2), and they are encouraged to keep on behaving as they have been doing, only more so (4:1, 10; 5:11). Also typical of pagan exhortation is the fact that the first part of the letter dwells on the friendly relations between writers and recipients, for it is within the context of friendship that admonition is best received. Like pagan moralists, too, the writers urge the Thessalonians to "imitate" personal models. Furthermore, there is much about the kind of life advocated here that would be familiar to the readers from their pre-Christian experience and from the world around them: "a quiet life," "minding one's own business," monogamy and sexual purity, special affection toward brothers (*philadelphia*), composure and the ability to comfort one another in the face of death (ch. 4)—all these are commonplaces in philosophical speeches and letters of the time.

However, most of these conventions receive a special twist in Paul's hands. The primary model to be imitated, for example, is "the Lord," who does not appear as a paradigm of familiar virtues —like Heracles the model of endurance or Penelope of faithfulness. Rather, he has a much more special role: one who died and was raised and will soon come again from heaven. The friendly relations recalled in the first three chapters center upon the recipients' conversion (1:9–10); they are not merely relations between individuals, but involve a community; and moreover they extend to other similar groups in the same province, in Achaia, and even in Judea (1:7–8; 2:14).

It is not until 4:1 that Paul begins directly to exhort the Thessalonian Christians, and there, too, he states most explicitly what is distinctive about the desired ethos. First, the exhortation is "in the Lord Jesus." This phrase not only invokes the authority of Jesus, implicit in the title "lord" and also in other phrases in the letter, like the precepts given "through the Lord Jesus" (4:2) and the declaration "by a word of the Lord" (4:15). It also signals a peculiar relationship that defines the social sphere within which these exhortations apply. Thus to be "in the Lord" connects the Thessalonian believers with "the churches of God in Christ Jesus" in other places (2:14) and with "the dead in Christ" who will be raised "through Jesus" and after the paradigm of God's raising Jesus, so that all together will "always be with the Lord" (4:13–18; cf. 5:10). The consolation of the bereaved thus rests on the claim that an extraordinary kind of communal life will transcend death, and that assertion is grounded in the shared belief "that Jesus died and rose again." Second, the object of the apostles' previous instruction and of this reminder is that the Christians should so behave as "to please God" (4:1).

"Pleasing God" is also at the center of Paul's description of his own behavior, which he sets before the readers as a model in 2:1–12. Moreover, he sharpens the meaning of that phrase by an antithesis —"pleasing God and not humans" (2:4), "not seeking glory from humans" (v. 6, my trans.)—and by specifying that the God he seeks to please is the one "who tests our hearts" (v. 4). Similarly he sums up his previous exhortations to the Thessalonians as urging them "to lead a life [literally, "to walk"] worthy of God, who calls you into his own kingdom and glory" (v. 12). In a society in which the "love of honor" (*philotimia*) was perhaps the most important sanction for public morality, the negation of "glory from humans" by "God's glory" is particularly pointed. (Yet Paul can use the verb cognate with *philotimia* in 4:11 to introduce a series of admonitions with which no one could quarrel.)

There is a certain absoluteness to the metaphor "pleasing God" because of its association with the verb Paul uses earlier, "to serve God (as a slave)" (1:9). The believer is called to please God as a slave pleases his master—a familiar concept in the religions of the ancient Near East and in the Bible, but rare in Greek or Roman religious sentiment. The metaphor occurs, moreover, in Paul's reminder of the Christians' conversion: they have "turned to God from idols" to be slaves of this "living and true God" (ibid.). Therefore their sexual behavior, for example, is to be marked by "holiness," unlike "the gentiles who do not know God" (4:4-7). Thus the peculiar way in which Paul talks about "pleasing God" distinguishes the standards of the *ekklēsia* from the mores of the larger society, just as similar language had helped Jews of Diaspora synagogues maintain their sense of uniqueness in a pagan world. Yet the line between is now drawn differently, for the people Paul addresses are themselves Gentiles, and the Christian groups in Thessalonica seem to have no connection at all with the synagogues there.

So, too, Paul uses the belief in an impending world judgment—so characteristic of Jewish apocalypticism—to reinforce the sense of absolute obligation to a sovereign who stands over against the prevailing human order. The God who is to be "served" and "pleased," who alone can confer "honor" that counts, is the "God who tests our hearts," whose "coming wrath" all must face (1:10). The time of this final judgment, for the Christians, is also the solemn advent (*parousia*) of the ruling "Lord," Jesus (see 1:10; 2:19; 5:9, 23; and note 4:6). As so often in apocalyptic literature, the eschatological images are used to distinguish the members of this community, "the sons of light and sons of the day," from "the rest" who are "of the night" and "in darkness" (5:5–8).

We see, then, a certain paradox in this letter. The specific moral expectations that Paul expresses, of the sort that one could state as moral rules, are hardly different from those widely accepted as "decent" in Greco-Roman society (note the admonition to behave "decently" in the view of "outsiders" in 4:12). Yet the overlaid theological warrants tend to emphasize distinctiveness and separation from the dominant society. "Holiness" is synonymous with "purity," and the metaphor implies separation: "not like the gentiles" (4:3–8).

The other side of the coin of separation is unusual emphasis on the solidarity and intimacy of the Christian fellowship. In a number of ways, some already mentioned, the rhetoric of this letter is so composed as to arouse the affection of the readers for one another, for the writers, and for Christian groups in other places with which they have had some direct or indirect connections. For example, Paul inserts a paragraph "On love of brothers" (4:9–12), a topic quite familiar in moral discourse of the day. Plutarch, for example, wrote a treatise with exactly this title. Plutarch's advice, however, concerned obligations between blood relatives, while in the Christian community every member was a brother or sister, for all were "children of God." More than a metaphor is involved here, for the Christians are evidently expected not only to cherish fellow members of the sect with the same care as they would natural siblings, but even to replace natural family ties by those of this new family of God, created by conversion and ritual initiation. That kind of deep resocialization was the norm not only in the Pauline mission circle but in other parts of the early Christian movement, too, as certain sayings of Jesus preserved in the Synoptic Gospels attest: "For I have come to set a man against his father, and a daughter against her mother, and a daughter-in-law against her mother-in-law" (Matt. 10:35; cf. v. 37 = Luke 14:26; Mark 3:31–35 and parallels).

The disruption of households was a charge that pagan opponents often leveled against Christianity, as against other new or foreign cults, and concern about replacement of family loyalties by this new "family of God" may have been one reason for the "affliction" and suffering of the Christians mentioned in this letter. Not only did pagan critics fear disruption of the traditional household, in the second and third centuries they sometimes complained about the excessive intimacy implied by the Christian habit of calling one another "brother" and "sister." Friendship was the proper context for a parenetic letter like 1 Thessalonians, and many features of the common topic "on friendship" do in fact appear in Paul's letter.[2] Yet he writes not to "friends" (as for example Epicurus did, to followers of his philosophy) but to "brothers," and he uses highly emotional language throughout. For example, the cliché found regularly in ancient letters, "absent in body but present in mind," is intensified by the addition, "We were bereft [lit. "orphaned," see above] of you," and by the reported emotions of "eagerness" and "great desire" to see the recipients (2:17). The latter words, and the equivalent verbs in 3:6, and indeed the whole mood of this section of the letter would have represented, in much of contemporary Hellenistic ethics, the kind of "passion" (*epithymia*, 2:17) of which the wise man ought to rid himself.

The requirement to obey God rather than human authorities and conventions was not alien to the Greek tradition—think of Socrates, especially as the Cynics remembered him. The "God who tests the heart," however, whom the Pauline Christian was taught to "serve," was not the internal *daimōn* of Socrates, which most of those who invoked his memory identified with human reason and the rational structure of nature. There is an emotional moment to the force of the Christian ethos which is not at all like the Platonic eros, let alone the high Stoic "passionlessness" (*apatheia*). And there is a self-conscious communal dimension of the sect's ethic which is far removed from the civic-mindedness of Greek ethics. Only among the Pythagoreans and the Epicureans, on the pagan side, and in Judaism could we find a similar emphasis on a community shaped for the moral instruction and admonition of its members (note the role of the leaders in 5:12–13, including prophets, vs. 19–20, but shared by all, vs. 11, 14–24).

Praise, Blame, and Exhortation: 1 Corinthians

The richest example of Christian parenesis that survives from the first century is 1 Corinthians, one of the extant portions of a long series of exchanges between Paul and the Christian groups of Corinth. When we read this letter, we see at once that Paul uses some of the same kinds of moral appeals as in 1 Thessalonians. The manner in which he introduces these appeals shows that the similarities stem not only from the habits of the same author, but from the fact that Paul and his coworkers have taught similar beliefs and rules to new Christians in both places. Some of the most prominent of the parallel themes are these:

God's will defines acceptable action. God, moreover, is understood as judge, and the context of judgment is eschatological.

The context for moral concern is the Christian community. As in 1 Thessalonians, the complementary terms which define what the community's character ought to be are its "holiness" and its unity. Holiness entails distinction from the "outside" society, though not absolute separation from it. The congregation's unity is grounded in the unity of Christ and expressed in mutual care and in self-limiting regard for others.

Personal examples, especially Christ and Paul, are prominent. More explicitly than in 1 Thessalonians, it is the crucifixion and resurrection of Jesus that become the structural model for understanding the apostle's experience and thence an extended metaphor to be used in making a variety of moral judgments.

It is also apparent that the variety and complexity of the action guides expressed or presumed by Paul in this letter are extraordinary. Even more striking than in 1 Thessalonians is the way in which Paul can mix together commonplaces of Greek and Roman moral rhetoric, arguments from Jewish scripture, and beliefs and rules peculiar to the Christian sect. For example, he can adopt the "catalogues of circumstances" that philosophers often used for self-defense or self-assertion, but in chapters 3 and 4 he merges these with the master image of the crucified Messiah. He can employ standard political wisdom about the unity and autonomy of a city, expressed in the commonplace allegory of the body and its limbs (in chapter 12), yet it is not the polis he is describing, but the company of "the holy ones"; the divisiveness is caused by different evaluations of ecstatic phenomena, construed as "gifts of the Spirit"; and the unity is derived from "the same Spirit, . . . the same Lord, . . . the same God" (12:4–6).

The complexity of the Corinthian correspondence obviously reflects a situation which is much more complicated than that of the Thessalonian Christians when Paul wrote them soon after their conversion. Even though no more than three or four years have gone by between Paul's founding of the congregations in Corinth and his writing of the first surviving letter, these congregations have moved further along on the road of institutionalization and self-reflection than had been the case in Thessalonica three years earlier. Among the general kinds of issues that are reflected in the particular problems which the letter addresses are these: (1) Conflicts over leadership, roles, and stratification within the community. The community is not so dependent on Paul as that at Thessalonica seemed still to be. Apollos' different style appealed to many Corinthian Christians, while their own local leaders, some with rather traditional roles (householders and patrons), others with novel, "charismatic" powers (prophets, tongue-speakers) vied with one another for leadership in the assemblies. The traditional structure of the Greco-Roman household asserted itself, since it was the context within which the Christian groups took shape, but it ran up against apparently contradictory values in the eschatological gospel and rituals of the sect. Were the roles of women, for example, and of slaves to be no different among those who were baptized into Christ, in whom "there is neither Jew nor Greek, . . . neither slave nor free, no male and female" (Gal. 3:28, RSV alt.)? Here the first issue touches on the other two. (2) Conflicts over the relation between the sect and the larger society of the colony Corinth. Must converts sever all ties with their former families and associates who had not become Christians? Could someone like Erastus, treasurer of the city (Rom. 16:23), continue to participate in the government of the colony without compromising his confession of Christ? Dare the Christians abandon the scruples about food that had protected the Jewish communities against assimilation, against contamination by the "idolatry" of pagan cults? (3) Practical consequences of the Christians' revolutionary "myth" of the crucified and resurrected Son of God. Baptized into his death and resurrection, initiated into the heavenly wisdom he brought, were the Christians now beyond good and evil, free from all constraints of customary morality, wherever the Spirit within them might lead?

Cultic Taboos, Elite Knowledge, and the Weaker Brother's Conscience

The texture of the moral issues discussed in 1 Corinthians will become clearer to us if we analyze one of them in some detail rather than surveying all. In 1 Corinthians 8–10 Paul is probably responding to the second of a series of questions that the Corinthians have put to him by letter (cf. 7:1). This question had to do with eating "idol-sacrifices"; that would include virtually all meat offered for sale in the public meat markets (10:25) or served by a pagan host at a dinner (10:27). For Jews in the Diaspora it was of utmost importance to avoid any participation in the cults of other deities than the One God of Israel. As we saw in 1 Thessalonians, the Christians shared that aversion. The book of Acts, written some three or four decades later than 1 Corinthians, reports that "Avoid meat offered to idols" was one of the firm rules for Gentile Christians formally laid down at the Apostolic Council in Jerusalem. Paul quotes a version of that rule in 1 Corinthians 10:14 just as he quotes the companion rule, "Avoid fornication," in 6:18 (compare Acts 15:20, 29; 21:25). Since he also quoted the latter rule in 1 Thessalonians 4:3 and presupposes it at 1 Corinthians 5:1 and 7:2, we might suppose that it is precisely the receipt of the "apostolic decree" by the Christians of Corinth that provoked their dispute and

Paul's reply. However, Paul's own discussion of the "Council" (in Gal. 2:1–10) mentions no such rules, and when he quotes the rules, he never hints that they had some "official" standing. Moreover, Revelation, written at around the same time as Acts, reveals that the issue was still arousing passions (Rev. 2:14, 20). It was thus not settled so neatly at the beginning of the Christian mission as the author of Acts would like us to believe. It is not surprising that in the Christian household groups of Corinth there was a division on the question.

Paul's own advice is by no means simple. He begins by quoting several terse statements, which sum up one side of the debate and may even be slogans used by that side's advocates. They may also have referred to the ones who disagreed with their "liberal" position as "the weak." When Paul later abstracted from this case some more general admonitions about relationships within the church (Rom. 14:1–15:13), he spoke of "the strong" and "the weak." There is good reason to suspect that the "strong" in Corinth belong to the wealthier and socially better placed minority of the Christian group (compare 1 Cor. 1:26). Perhaps, as many modern scholars have argued, "the strong" Christians had developed some complex ideology—an early form of Gnosticism, for example, or some mystical interpretation of baptism and spirit-possession—but we do not have to imagine anything so elaborate in order to understand the argument of these three chapters. The "strong" say, "We all have knowledge [*gnōsis*]," and what they know is that "There is no idol in the world" and "There is no God but One" (8:1, 4, my trans.). This knowledge gives freedom and power. Pagan satirists sometimes poked fun at religious scrupulosity; "the superstitious man" was a stock comic character. Jewish writers had been satirizing the use of images ("idols") in other cults for centuries. The "knowledge" of the "strong" Christian liberated him at a stroke not only from superstition and from all cultic scruples, but even from the Jewish fear of "idolatry." He can, in short, go wherever he is invited, eat whatever he likes.

Paul does not contradict these statements, but sets qualifications against them: "Knowledge inflates; love builds." And, cryptically, "If anyone imagines that he knows something, he does not yet know as he ought to know." In 8:7 Paul does contradict the "all" of v. 1: not "all" have this knowledge that nihilates the dangerous world of religious taboos. By saying "we *all* have knowledge," the "strong" deny the existence of those "weak" Christians, ignorant and superstitious, who still scruple at "idolatry." Paul will not permit that denial: "Take care lest this liberty of yours somehow become a stumbling block to the weak" (v. 9). Paul's rhetorical strategy here disrupts the smooth logic of the strong Christians whose premises he accepts. The nihilation of paganism's symbols, their exposure as human fantasy, is interrupted at the point where it threatens the integrity of the Christian who has not yet grasped that liberating insight. That person, and not just the symbolic world of paganism, is now in danger of being "destroyed," and at that point Paul names him not "the weak" but "the brother for whom Christ died" (v. 11).

One could, accordingly, sum up the main point of these three chapters by paraphrasing 8:9–11: "Do not let the exercise of your liberating knowledge harm your brother or sister." Paul's own summary, at the end of chapter 10, contains a similar statement in rule form: "Let no one seek his own (good) but the (good) of the other" (10:24, my trans.). To extract this rule from the dialectic of these chapters, however, would flatten and impoverish the effective grammar of the moral process in which Paul and the two factions at Corinth were engaged.

What is characteristic of that grammar is a double movement: affirmation and reversal. That pattern becomes even more vivid in chapters 9 and 10. In chapter 9 Paul presents his own behavior as an example. That is a common procedure in parenesis, but the way he does so is anything but common. More than half the chapter is an elaborate argument that apostles are to receive financial support from those whom they evangelize. Paul sets out more than a half dozen quite different warrants for this rule: the prominent examples of the other apostles, the Lord's brother, and Cephas (9:4–6); the secular analogies of shepherds and soldiers (v. 7); an argument from scripture, in the manner that later rabbis would call *midrash aggadah* (vs. 9–11); the logic of reciprocal obligation (v. 11); a simple analogy from scripture (v. 13); and finally an explicit directive from the Lord (Jesus) (v. 14)—not to mention minor supports, like the proverb in v. 10. Yet all of this argument is only in order to set in relief the reversal: "Nevertheless, we have not made use of this right" (v. 12b, reiterated in 15). The word translated "right" here is the same as that translated "liberty" in 8:9, so the point of the example is clear. The apostle exercises his liberty by choosing not to use it; so ought the "strong." Further on, Paul states the reversal even more dramatically: "For even though I am free from all, I have made myself a slave to all" (9:19).

Yet the warrant for the reversal is not so clear. The first explanation is ironic, almost jocular: Paul refuses pay so that he can have *something* to boast about—since he is so compelled to preach the gospel that he cannot boast about that; his wage is that he takes no wages (9:15–18). More serious is his statement about flexibility as a missionary strategy (19–23); finally he presents the commonplace analogy from athletics: winning requires self-discipline (24–27). None of these really explains why Paul does not exercise the right he has so carefully defended. He is merely presenting himself as example; all the rest is for emphasis. However, the reader who recalls the early chapters of the letter will understand that there is an unstated warrant for the non-use of power, and Paul will mention it again at the end of this argument: it is the model furnished by the crucified Messiah (see 11:1).

Paul has not finished complicating the life of the "strong" Christian. In chapter 10 he provides a learned support for the position of the "weak," in the form of a homily or midrash based on Exodus 32:6. The episode of the Golden Calf recounted in that verse was, in Jewish tradition as in scripture itself, the classic instance of Israel's idolatry—at the very moment when Moses was receiving the Torah (repository of all worthwhile knowledge) and immediately after Israel was liberated from Egypt. Paul does not derive a new rule from this midrash, which he or someone else had evidently composed earlier, but uses it as backing for the common early Christian rule, "Flee from idolatry" (10:14, my trans.). Moreover, he seems further to undercut the liberating knowledge of the "strong" by insisting that the pagan gods do after all have some real existence: they are "demons" (v. 20). One cannot partake of the cup and table of the Lord and also of cultic meals honoring "demons" (v. 21).

Yet there is still another reversal. After siding so vigorously with the anti-idolators of the Corinthian church, Paul returns to the slogans of the strong, and to the qualifications he had made at the beginning: Liberty, yes, but only if it is "advantageous," if it "builds up"; the rule of thumb is, Let each seek the other's welfare (vs. 23–24). But then: "Eat whatever is sold in the meat market without raising any question on the ground of conscience," backed by a scriptural text! And vs. 27–30 apply the rule to the specific case of invitations to dinner.

The practical result is a compromise, and perhaps it worked to ease the tensions between the people of different status in the Corinthian church—we have no way of knowing. The process that led to this result, however, is not compromise but the peculiar dialectic of affirmations and reversals just described. Nor would we grasp what is most important about that dialectic were we to see in it only the ingenuity of Paul's rhetoric. It is true that we see the situation only through Paul's eyes, but his genius is that his dialectical rhetoric subsumes and articulates a process in which conflicting factions of the congregation were trying to discover an appropriate manner of life. On the one side is the brilliant discovery that Jewish-Christian monotheism has the potential to desacralize the everyday world, a discovery that nicely serves the interests of a few socially elevated members of the group by permitting them to ignore the religious dimensions of civic life. (Erastus the city treasurer, mentioned in Rom. 16:23—probably the same man who a few years later was Market Commissioner—would find his conscience much relieved.) On the other side is the experience of the many people of very little power, for whom the firm stance against "idolatry" learned by so many generations of Jews in the Diaspora seemed an indispensable defense for the Christian groups as well, against a world filled with uncanny powers. Paul uses the mediating symbol of Jesus crucified, not to achieve a theoretical synthesis of these opposing positions, but to signify a way in which the persons who occupied the positions could understand their engagement with one another. The grammar of this moral process is the logic of the interaction that Paul undertakes to bring about. In that process meet three different but overlapping perceptions of the world—that of "the weak," that of "the strong," and Paul's—each informed by the distinctive experiences, history, and social location of the different parties, but each transformed in its own special way by the novel Christian teachings as those persons appropriated them.

Messianic Biography as Community-forming Literature: The Gospel of Matthew

All four of the canonical Gospels, it seems now, were written for readers who were already Christians. That does not mean that they do not contain some elements of basic instruction about Christianity. A didactic purpose is most obvious in the two-volume history Luke-Acts; for example, in the preface addressed to one Theophilus. Even there, however, the author writes that he wants to explain things in which Theophilus has already been instructed. In the case of Matthew, which will serve as our sample, it is even more evident that the book was composed to reinforce and modify the beliefs and commitment of Christians rather than to initiate them.

Obviously, too, "Matthew," like the other evangelists, is interested in forming and reforming Christian behavior as well as beliefs and attitudes. For example, the warnings at the conclusion of the Sermon on the Mount stress behavioral tests: of "false prophets," to be known "by their fruits"; of itinerant charismatics, whose prophecies, miracles, and exorcisms count for nothing, but only doing "the will of [the] Father" (Matt. 7:15–23). The parable of the wise and foolish builders makes the same point: the wise person is the one "who hears these words of mine *and does them*" (7:24–27, emphasis added). The point is made also by the stress throughout this Gospel on "righteousness," which must, for example, exceed that of the scribes and Pharisees (5:20). The depiction of the Final Judgment in 25:31–46 confirms the importance of right action.

Furthermore, there are ample hints throughout this Gospel that the author writes for specific groups of Christians with their own special history, and in a situation in which certain specific issues are under debate. Unfortunately it is not so easy to infer the outlines of that situation and those issues from this kind of literature as it is in the case of letters. Nevertheless, some features of Matthew's community are tolerably clear. He writes in Greek to a Greek-speaking church, probably in an eastern city; most scholars think this was the great metropolis of Antioch in Syria, sometime in the last quarter of the first century. There may have been many small household groups of Christians in Antioch at that time, however, and quite likely there was a certain diversity among them. Not all may have shared the history and perspectives that Matthew assumes.

Matthew's Christians have been very close to the Jews of the land of Israel, and specifically to those "scribes and Pharisees" who were engaged in reconstituting Israel's institutions and piety after the destruction of the Temple in A.D. 70. The rivalry between these Christians and those leaders who "love . . . being called rabbis" (23:6–7) has turned hostile (see, e.g., the whole of Matt. 23), and by the time of writing the separation between Matthew's groups and the Jewish communities is complete. There remains within the Christian groups, however, an active debate over the role of "law" and "commandments" in shaping faithful response to God and, more generally, over the right way for Jesus' followers to appropriate the heritage of Israel.

Further, there is dissension within Matthew's communities over different sources and modes of authority. On the one hand, we see clear signs of the development of formal—institutional and legal—kinds of authority; on the other, the "charismatic" power of prophets is still acknowledged, though with some ambivalence. Traditions of Jesus, both stories about his life and his pronouncements and parables, play an important role in these discussions.

The vehicle that Matthew and the other evangelists chose for affecting the behavior of their communities is different from the parenetic letters at which we have just looked. Narrative is a less direct mode of instruction and admonition. Now the use of narrative, especially of biography, to provide moral lessons and examples was quite familiar in the literature of the time—one need only recall, from a few years later than Matthew, the "Lives" by Plutarch. Didactic biography was a specifically Hellenistic genre; the Jews who used it (Philo, for the most prominent example) were Greek-speaking, and we have no extended examples in extant Hebrew or Aramaic literature of the time.[3] However, the way Matthew uses the story of Jesus to instruct his readers is rather different from Plutarch and his like.

Jesus as Wise Moral Teacher

One of Matthew's strategies is to depict Jesus as a teacher of wisdom, that is, a figure something like Ben Sira (see above, chapter 3). This portrait had already taken shape, to a certain extent, among those who collected and compiled Jesus' aphorisms, parables, and other wise sayings, and Matthew expanded on that portrait, even as he wove one such collection into his Gospel. He has gathered many of the sayings into speeches set on five different occasions in Jesus' career; the first of these is the Sermon on the Mount (Matt. 5–7).

The Sermon on the Mount serves as an *epitomē* or summary of Jesus' teaching. In similar fashion, both in Jewish and in Greco-Roman tradition, the philosopher sets before his hearers a way of ethical living that leads to "happiness."[4] The "beatitudes" or "makarisms," a form familiar in Jewish wisdom literature, are thus a fitting introduction. A reader familiar with popular philosophies of the day would find much here in common with Cynic teaching: simplicity of life and speech, boldness and defenselessness, readiness to defy public conventions. The terms of discourse, however, are explicitly Jewish. The Law and the Prophets must be fulfilled, exceeding the righteousness of scribes and Pharisees (5:17–20). One must imitate the perfection of God (5:48) and expect his reward.

Not only is the ethic epitomized here Jewish, it is sectarian—that is, it requires a deliberate choice to follow the authority of Jesus and not that of other Jewish leaders and teachers. That requirement is suggested already by the setting in 5:1: Jesus addresses "his disciples," although "the crowds" are also present and respond in 7:28–29.

The opposition to other traditions is most explicit in six antithetical statements in ch. 5, which take the form "You have heard that it was said, X, but I say to you, Y." A closer look shows that these statements are of two kinds. Three of them contain sayings found also in Luke (on divorce, 5:32 = Luke 16:18; on nonretaliation, 5:39–41 = Luke 6:29–30; on loving enemies, 5:44–47 = Luke 6:27–35); evidently these are drawn from the common collection of Jesus' sayings that both evangelists used. The parallels in Luke, however, do not have the antithetic form; Matthew has rewritten these sayings, giving them the form that he found in the other three antitheses. These latter he most likely took from the special traditions of his own community, perhaps from the wandering charismatics toward whom Matthew shows such ambivalence. Each of these unique antitheses interprets one of the Ten Commandments: "You shall not kill," "You shall not commit adultery," and "You shall not swear falsely." And the saying of Jesus in each case radicalizes the commandment by applying it not to a legally definable public violation (murder, adultery, perjury), but to dispositions: anger, lust, any weakness of absolute integrity that might need the prop of an oath. It is not quite accurate to say that this move internalizes the norms, for the examples of violations are all relational and are overtly expressed. It is clear that this is a perfectionist ethic, and that it is sectarian in the sense that such requirements are expressly set over against the ordinary demands of the Torah upon everyone. In similar fashion the Essenes radicalized the commandments; indeed two of these same rules appear in their literature or reports about them —they forebade both oaths and expressions of anger toward fellows.[5]

Matthew incorporates this sectarian form, and he uses it to reshape other rules which he drew from the common collection. Yet what results from this reshaping (5:31–32, 38–42, 43–47) is different from the older antitheses. Here the rules based on the Torah are not deepened, but reversed. The time when the concession of divorce is allowed is over (cf. 19:8); the rule "Eye for eye, tooth for tooth" is superseded; and the negative implication of "Love your neighbor [alone] as yourself," canceled. What is emphasized is thus the contrast between the conventional interpretation of the commandments and Jesus' revision. What the two kinds of antitheses share in Matthew's composition is the perfectionism of all (5:48). The sectarian character of the ethic consists in the demand that prudential and publicly enforceable rules be set aside altogether. The only valid standard is "the will of the Father in heaven." How is that standard to be ascertained?

The "will of the Father" is not an abstract perfection, for the rules laid down here belong to the realm of everyday: marriage, truth-telling, facing foreign soldiers and other enemies, giving alms, praying, forgiving people, fasting. There is no clear line between sacred and secular. On the other hand, Matthew provides no code of behavior. Although the risen Jesus in Matthew directs that new disciples must be taught "to observe all that I have commanded you" (28:20), we have here no system of commandments. The rules are exemplary not comprehensive, pointers to the kind of life expected in the community, but not a map of acceptable behavior. Still less does Matthew's Jesus state philosophical principles from which guidelines for behavior could be rationally derived. We are left with the puzzle that while Jesus plays the role of a conventional sage in Matthew, his teachings recorded here do not add up to an ethical system. It is not in such a program of teachings, apparently, that Matthew understands the will of God to be discovered.

It may be significant that "teacher" and "rabbi" are titles not used of Jesus in Matthew by committed disciples, but only by outsiders, opponents, and his betrayer.[6] In order to achieve the "righteousness" Matthew demands, members of his community need to know much more than Jesus' collected teachings. From this Gospel we can deduce some of the things they did know: the story of Jesus' career, told with pathos and mystery in Mark's Gospel; the ascetic, spirit-possessed prophets who wandered into their city, imitating Jesus' poverty, homelessness, and detachment and guided only by his image and his spirit that spoke within them; the ordered assembly with its elders, its powers to "bind and loose," its "scribe[s] trained for the kingdom of heaven" who by their careful study of scripture knew how to draw from the Jewish treasure "what is new and what is old." The writer has brought all these together, but in the composite it is the narrative that dominates.

Jesus as Israel's Messiah and Founder of the New People

The first words of the book make evident the author's purpose to awaken some very special memories in knowledgeable readers: *biblos geneseōs,* "book of genesis." That is the name by which Greek readers knew the first book of Jewish scripture, in which this phrase appears (e.g., Gen. 5:1). The genealogy of Jesus, which follows in Matthew, connects him by a carefully arranged pattern with the great epochs of the biblical history: Abraham, David, the Babylonian exile. Succeeding elements in the birth story reinforce this impression. Events occur "in order that what was spoken through the prophet might be fulfilled." The repetition of details familiar from the biblical stories or their elaboration in popular lore link this one "born king of the Jews" with Abraham, Moses, Israel in Egypt, the exodus and Sinai, and so on. Some of these motifs—dreams, astrological portents, conflict with tyrants—were common trappings of Hellenistic biographies of extraordinary individuals and are therefore appropriate stylistic devices to emphasize that Jesus is "the one called 'Anointed' " (1:16, my trans.). However, their principal function here is to suggest a predestined plan that all participants in these events were obliged to follow, a plan continuous with the sacral history of Israel.

Continuity is not the only note sounded here, however. The massacre of children by Herod, in his vain attempt to eliminate the young rival, not only recalls the story of Moses, it also foreshadows the crucifixion of "the King of the Jews." Thus Matthew invests his narrative with that same pathos which he found in his model, the Gospel of Mark, but he does so in a very different way. In this Gospel the rising conflict will ultimately set Jesus not only against the leaders of Israel but against "all the people," who are made to answer Pilate, "His blood be on us and on our children" (27:25). Matthew's picture of history has evidently been shaped both by the common Christian memory of Jesus' crucifixion and also by this particular community's conflicts with the reorganized Jewish communities in postwar Palestine and Syria.

We get another hint of Matthew's sense of history in the instructions to the Twelve in chapter 10. One might think that the manner of life prescribed here—poverty, mendicancy, homelessness—are being set forth as ideals for discipleship in Matthew's church. Such an ascetic life became the norm in eastern parts of Syria at a later time, and perhaps the itinerant prophets mentioned several times in Matthew already represented that life in Matthew's city.[7] Certainly not all the instructions given by Jesus to the Twelve are binding on Matthew's community, however. The restriction of the mission to Israel alone (10:5–6) is explicitly removed in 28:19. Further, Matthew has lifted 10:17–22 from Jesus' apocalyptic prediction of future disturbances in Mark 13:9–13. The changed context has the effect of removing the predicted difficulties from the reader's future, placing them in the community's past experience. Verses 40–42, moreover, emphasize the reward for those who receive the wanderers, not for the wanderers themselves. Discipleship in Matthew is not identical with imitation of the ascetic life of Jesus or his twelve special missionaries. Thus, for all the church's inevitable retrojection of its own experiences into the time of Jesus, this author does find ways to accord to the past an integrity of its own.

It is not only a model for the present but also a basis which is different from the present and which therefore requires different responses.

The narrative of Matthew is thus something more than setting and backing for Jesus' teachings. The Teacher is also the Messiah, who cares for, heals, calls, and transforms his people. He is also the Judge, the Son of Man who as God's agent exercises the Final Judgment on all humankind. The relationship of the Christian groups to this Messiah/Son-of-Man/Son-of-God is modeled by the course of discipleship described in the narrative, but there is also an awareness that new occasions teach new duties.

It is instructive to compare the ethics of Matthew with that of the Qumran Essenes (see chapter 3, above). Both are ethics for communities that understand their own existence as results of extraordinary interventions of God at the End of Days. They perceive those extraordinary events to be fulfillment of scriptural prophecies, which could not be rightly understood before the new revelations. Both sects were founded by righteous, spirit-inspired teachers, who were persecuted by the Jerusalem leaders. Both believe that they, and not the established authorities of the Jewish community, are the true heirs of the biblical promises and the truly obedient people of God's kingdom. Both wait for vindication in the near future, when God will send his Messiah(s) and angels to defeat and judge wickedness and to transform the world into his righteous kingdom. Both believe that the inner life of the sect must be a life which is, in a preliminary way, fit for that kingdom. And, while "commandments" are of great importance to both communities, the rules that are actually stated are only exemplary rather than comprehensive, and aim more at reminding the members of the community's intensive claims than at providing universal moral guidelines. In both cases the community as such is trusted with the power of deciding and guiding moral questions.

The differences, to be sure, are also substantial. The eschatological timetable in Matthew is much more advanced than in the Qumran documents; the Messiah has come, and it is his return in power that is awaited. The Roman destruction of the Temple in Jerusalem is seen as proof of God's judgment against those who persecuted the Messiah. The new people to whom the kingdom is to be given is already in existence. Moreover, that new people is no longer restricted to the faithful remnant of Israel, but is directed to make disciples from "all the nations." There are differences, too, in the moral temper of the community's rules; for example, a stress upon unlimited forgiveness, where Qumran's ordinances stress rigor.

Perhaps the most important difference, however, is precisely in the characteristic form of the literature produced by each group. Both produce rulebooks, reinterpretations of scripture, exhortations, apocalypses. From Qumran, however, we have no biography, no "gospel." We do not know even the name of the Righteous Teacher. Of his career we know only shadowy outlines of a couple of events that can be reconstructed from the biblical commentaries. The person vanishes behind the organization he founded and the interpretations of prophecy and Torah that his followers continued. Not so the Jesus of Matthew. Mark had made his story the "gospel" itself, the proclamation of eschatological good news. Matthew makes that story part of the grammar of Christian ethics. The commandments are not separable from the commander, the teachings from the teacher. Discipleship is "following" the person identified in the story, who, raised from the dead, goes on leading the community. It is therefore possible to ask not only what *did* Jesus say, but what *does* he now wish his people to do—a sort of inquiry that obviously produced considerable dissension among the prophets and other leaders of the Matthean community.

There is indeed an uneasy tension in this gospel, as there must have been in the Christian communities of its time and place. The rigorist imitators of Jesus' ascetic life have their say, but it is countered by the parables that warn against premature attempts to purify the church. The tension is not resolved, but suspended. All must face judgment by the Son of Man, and all will be surprised, for neither a literalist imitation of his life-style, nor a rigorist obedience of his words as law, nor a charismatic appropriation of his miraculous power is any guarantee of faithfulness. Yet it is those whose actions are in accord with the character of that same Son of Man as rendered by this narrative, and with the plan of God in which he is the protagonist, who find themselves among the sheep on the right hand.

On the Side of the Angels: The Apocalypse

The imagery of the Revelation to John is so phantasmagoric, its scale so cosmic, that a connection with human morality may seem remote at best. Yet apocalypses are literature of moral passion, and this one is no exception. It is a letter addressed to churches in seven cities of the province Asia (in the southwest corner of modern Turkey), and its purpose is certainly to affect the behavior of those who hear it read in their meetings (Rev. 1:3; 22:6–20).

The general strategy of the Apocalypse is to oppose to the ordinary view of reality, as anyone might experience it in Smyrna or Laodicea, a quite different picture of the world as seen from the standpoint of heaven. The visionary conventions of apocalyptic literature serve this strategy well, for the letter purports to convey the contents of a continuous vision experienced by the author, a certain prophet named John, while "in the Spirit on the Lord's Day," that is, in a trance state. Within the vision itself, after preliminary instructions about each of the seven churches, John is transported up into the heavenly throne room, where he sees God seated in imperial splendor, surrounded by his court. From that vantage point, he and his readers are permitted to see the ensuing events that unfold in both heaven and earth.

In the view from heaven, Rome is the center of the earthly world and absolutely dominates all aspects of its life. Her wealth, power, and luxury are voluptuously portrayed, albeit with disgust, in chapters 17 and 18. For another example of so grand a conception of Rome's universal dominance of commerce, culture, and government, one would have to turn to the famous speech in her praise by another provincial writer, Aelius Aristides (see above, chapter 1). Incidentally, Aristides, a generation later than John, spent much of his life in Smyrna and Pergamum, two of the cities to which John writes. For the average resident of those cities, including the average Christian, Rome's power was no doubt well known, but hardly a matter of daily concern. The ordinary life of plain people in Smyrna, Pergamum, Thyatira, and the rest went on without much visible effect from Rome. As for Christians, there is virtually no evidence for any organized persecution of them in Asia, other than the hints in Revelation itself. Aristides' view was that of a wealthy and ambitious cosmopolitan; John's that of a prophet who saw Rome as the Enemy.

Not only is she the enemy of the Christians, Rome is revealed in chapter 13 as a "beast" controlled by the "ancient serpent," the primeval enemy of God. Hence the description of the empire of God and the empire of Rome in these visions strangely mirror each other. To the Great Whore, who is "the great city which has dominion over the kings of the earth," corresponds the Bride of the Lamb, "clothed with fine linen, bright and pure" (19:8), who is "the holy city, new Jerusalem," which descends from heaven (21:2–22:5). On the one side is the One "who is and who was and who is to come" (1:4, 8; 4:8; 11:17; 16:5); on the other the Beast who "was and is not and is to come" (17:8, 11). The Lamb stands "as though it had been slain" (*hōs esphagmenos,* 5:6); the second Beast has a head that "seemed to have a mortal wound *(hōs esphagmenē),* but its mortal wound was healed" (13:3). Angels and prophets are found on both sides, as are armies. The servants of God are sealed on their foreheads (7:2–10), and the Beast requires that everyone be marked on hand or brow, without which no one can buy or sell (13:16–17). And the imperial grandeur of God's throne and court, while the imagery is largely drawn from older biblical depictions and ultimately from common ancient Near Eastern ways of envisioning the highest deity, stands tacitly but obviously over against all the pomp of the Roman emperor. Domitian's self-exaltation was an object of silent disapproval by many in Rome, to judge from the outpouring of criticism by many writers after his death; some of his flatterers, those critics said, had called him *dominus et deus*, "lord and god."

If we were to describe John's prophecy in conventional literary terms, then, we would say that he has made his description of the heavenly reality a parody on the power and ceremony of Rome. The effect upon the reader, however, is just the contrary: Rome is presented as a parody of heaven. Its pomp is sham, its order a diabolical artifice, its power a bold front concealing its predestined destruction. Numerous oxymorons, that is, sharply paradoxical expressions, as well as explicit inversions in John's language hint to the reader that things are often the opposite of what they seem: the Lion of Judah turns out to be a lamb, and he stands as though slaughtered. And this slain lamb-lion has power to do what "a strong angel" cannot manage (ch. 5). Like the Lamb, those who are slain by the forces of the beasts "conquer." They wash their robes white in blood (7:14). Among the Christians themselves, there are some who think they are rich, "not knowing that you are wretched, pitiable, poor, blind, and naked" (3:17), while others who seem powerless will receive obeisance from those they fear (3:8–9), and some who suffer poverty are really rich (2:9). The business of this writing is to stand things on their heads in the perceptions of its audience, to rob the established order of the most fundamental power of all: its sheer facticity.

The moral strategy of the Apocalypse, therefore, is to destroy common sense as a guide for life. Prudential morality is based on the taken-for-granted consensus about the way things are. Rome, for example, is a fact of such magnitude that it is unlikely to be altered. For a century she has represented peace and stability in the provinces; so long as one does not disturb the public order or willfully affront one of the symbols or agents of her sovereignty, Rome is a powerful but benign presence. That is the common sense and from it follows a quiet and peaceable life. The vision of the Apocalypse shreds and rips away that common sense with as much violence as that with which John sees the sky itself removed. But what kind of life follows, if the reversed images and torn language of John succeed?

The whole Apocalypse is implicitly hortatory and it contains many explicit exhortations. Yet it names surprisingly few specific sins to be avoided or virtues to be cultivated, and even these are usually expressed so metaphorically or so generally that almost any known moral rule could be included. Righteous judgment is the principal theme of the second half of the book, and the judgment comes against all the earth and its inhabitants, with the sole exception of the "servants of God" (7:3). Thus the stress is not upon particular sins of individuals that are judged, but on a universal corruption from which only a few are redeemed.

Military images abound in John's depiction of "what must soon take place," but the active combatants are principally superhuman: Christ and the angels against the forces of the great dragon. The metaphoricity of their combat is also emphasized by some of the (biblical) language: Christ conquers by "the sword of his mouth" and by his sacrifice as the slain Lamb. The humans who "conquer" do so by remaining faithful, perhaps also to the point of death, not by taking up arms against the government. The Revelation is no call for revolutionary action, but for passive resistance, for disengagement and quietism.

So the virtues named in the assessments of individual churches in chapters 2 and 3 are work, labor, endurance under stress, love—but hatred for deviants. The only specific vices mentioned are tolerance for false teaching and the vices that the teachers are said to teach: fornication and eating sacrificed meat (2:14, 20). Fornication may be a metaphor for idolatry, as it so often is in the biblical prophets, or it may refer to any kind of sexuality deemed illicit. Most sexual images in Revelation are quite negative, and so are all the female figures except for the pregnant woman of chapter 12 and the Bride of the Lamb. The retinue of the Lamb are 144,000 male virgins "who have not defiled themselves with women" (14:4). This latter motif, however, is perhaps derived from the ancient rules of "holy war" in Israel and need not represent a literal requirement of sexual asceticism in the Asian churches. That John detests the woman prophet whom he calls "Jezebel" is apparent, but that may not be because he rejects leadership by women, but only because of what she teaches. He does, after all, also speak of "Balaam," whose teachings are equivalent (2:14).

What these other prophets teach that is so abhorrent to the prophet John is a relaxed attitude toward the surrounding (pagan) culture. Their position may be likened to that of the "strong" Christians of Corinth a generation earlier. John would have despised them, but he would despise Paul's dialectical middle ground even more. It is precisely the middle ground which his dualistic prose annihilates. It is the "lukewarm," he believes, who make God vomit (3:16). Assimilation to the culture of the Roman provincial cities arouses a divine nausea in John; separation is what is wanted. He is particularly clear that one result will be economic deprivation. The entanglement of most of the world with Rome is above all economic; it is the sea captains and the merchants, especially of luxury goods, who will howl most disconsolately at Rome's burning (ch. 18). Lydia the purple-seller (Acts 16:14), if she were still alive and returned to her native Thyatira, would have to go begging if John had his way. Wealth itself, especially commercial wealth, seems a vice: "no one can buy or sell unless he has the mark, that is, the name of the beast or the number" (Rev. 12:17).

The demand laid on the Christians who are here addressed is thus an unconditional loyalty to the one side in the vast, unseen struggle between cosmic powers that is occurring or about to occur. There is no room for compromise—no benign acceptance of meat in an unbeliever's home, no undefiling commerce—or a "lukewarm" response. It is a time for "witnessing," which can lead to death (as for Antipas, 2:13). In compensation, the faithful are under the protection of God and his angels. The little Christian cells in the Asian cities are dwarfed by the cosmic battle that unfolds in John's vision, but they are ultimately safe, he insists, if they will merely "hold fast."

A Handbook (Revised): The *Didache*

In each of the samples of early Christian moral teaching or exhortation we have looked at so far, there is a strong authorial voice—of the founding apostle, the evangelist, the visionary prophet—imposed upon the traditional materials that each writer gathered and used. This is not always the case in early Christian literature, however. Beginning early in the second century, Christians began to put together collections of miscellaneous rules for behavior and for governance of churches; modern scholars call these "church order literature." Sometimes these, too, were carefully composed, often in the name of an apostle; examples are the canonical First Letter to Timothy and the Letter to Titus, which were put forth in Paul's name, and the epistle widely attributed to Barnabas in antiquity; the genuine letter of Bishop Polycarp to the Philippian Christians contains much of the same kind of material. Other such collections, however, seem to have "evolved" (as Robert Kraft has put it) by a continuous process of revision, addition, and rearrangement. When we look at one of these collections, we may be closer to the way a novice in the Christian faith would have been introduced to the Christian life than when we read the more literarily whole writings.

Often the "church order" manuals were given titles like *The Teaching of the Twelve Apostles, The Apostolic Tradition,* or the like. That is true of the one we shall here consider, which was rediscovered in a manuscript in Constantinople just over a century ago. In that manuscript, which also contained the *Epistle of Barnabas* and some other writings, this work is called *Teaching of the Twelve Apostles,* and it is commonly known by the first word of this title in Greek, *Didachē.* The manuscript also gives an alternate title, or subtitle: "The Lord's Teaching to the Gentiles Through the Twelve Apostles."

Since publication of the new discovery in 1883, fragments of the *Didache* have been found on papyrus, as well as evidence both of its translation into other languages in antiquity (one copy of a Georgian version survived until the first part of this century) and of its reuse by later writers of church orders. Analysis of the *Didache* has shown that it, in turn, had reused earlier materials, some of which it shared in one form or another with *Barnabas,* with a third-century Latin document called *Doctrina XII Apostolorum,* and perhaps with some other early writings. And the *Didache* itself underwent some additions and revisions between its first compilation in this form and that version which we now have. The present state of the evidence does not permit certainty about the exact sequence of all these writings and revisions, but it does suffice to give us a picture of a long period of active and widespread employment of the kind of material we have in the *Didache.* What we have in this document, then, is something like one frame out of a moving picture, a slice from an ongoing tradition that was constantly being revised. The date of our "still" is around the middle of the second century or a little later; the place is uncertain, though the commonest guess is Alexandria.[8]

The *Didache* begins, "There are two ways, one of life and one of death; and between the two ways there is a great difference." The metaphor of two paths, one of virtue the other of vice, was a commonplace in ancient parenesis. In the Greek world the most popular version was a fable of Prodicus about Heracles at a road fork. The image was equally popular with Jews, who could recall the words of Jeremiah 21:8, among other passages: "Thus says the LORD: Behold, I set before you the way of life and the way of death." And

Jeremiah, in turn, may have alluded to Deuteronomy 30:19: "I have set before you life and death, blessing and curse; therefore choose life." We have met a similar formulation above (chapter 3) in the "Rule of the Community" from Qumran. There, however, the paths are called "the way of light and the way of darkness," and that is how most of the early Christian versions, including *Barnabas* and the *Doctrina,* described them, too. The compiler (or one of the compilers) of the *Didache* prefers the biblical language of Life and Death.

Choice is the immediate implication of the figure. You must choose. Moreover, the form of the trope imposes upon the choice a single pair of alternatives: this way or that. Not, as experience might have suggested to us, one way out of three or a half dozen. And the choice itself is single: one path or the other, and no cutting across if you change your mind later, for "There is a great difference between the Two Ways." Other versions of the Two Ways emphasize the sharpness of this division and the weight of this choice by informing us that there are spirits or angels in charge of each path, and judgment at the end. The *Epistle of Barnabas,* for example, says: "Over one are appointed light-bearing angels of God, but over the other, angels of Satan" (18.1d), and concludes: "For this reason there is resurrection, for this reason there is recompense" (21.1c).[9] Both features are very much like the language of the Two Ways in the Essene Rule, where we read of "two spirits" appointed to rule the Two Ways, and the "visitation" of each at the end of days. By calling the two paths "Death" and "Life," the *Didache* hints at the portentousness of the moral decision, and the handbook closes, as we shall see, with a warning of judgment. Nevertheless, the *Didache*'s version of the Two Ways omits the superhuman antagonists and at its conclusion sounds a much milder note of judgment: "If you can bear the Lord's full yoke, you will be perfect. But if you cannot, then do what you can" (6.2).

A modest ethic, this. We can understand how someone would have thought it appropriate for beginners in the faith and thus added it to instructions for baptism, the Eucharist, and other aspects of church life: "Baptize as follows, when you have rehearsed the aforesaid teaching" (7.1, trans. Kraft). We may reasonably feel that the catechumens must have been taught a great deal else besides, for there is nothing overtly Christian in chapters 1–6. Indeed, many students of the *Didache* think that with the exception of 1.3b–6, which are a pastiche of aphorisms from the Gospels of Matthew and Luke and from other sources, these chapters were a Jewish catechism that Christians simply took over. Be that as it may, the contents are rather miscellaneous. We have a collection of moral rules-of-thumb. Within each small group of similar type, there is some rhetorical logic, but no repeated pattern of any considerable scope. There is no systematic way of deriving action guides, nor is there an attempt at a comprehensive listing of all the rules one would need, nor is there a hierarchical ordering of the rules that are given. There is even some inconsistency. For example, about charity, 4.5–8 is rather more generous than 1.5–6!

There are, to be sure, some points of emphasis even in this much-worked-over version of the Two Ways. The "Way of Life" begins, as it did in the version known also to "Barnabas" and the author of the *Doctrina,* "First, you must love God who made you, and second, your neighbor as yourself" (1.2). That summary of the Commandments, which appears very often in early Jewish and Christian literature, thus becomes a guide for the reader, implicitly unpacked by the "commandments" that follow. None of the compilers of the *Didache* have taken the two commandments as headings for further development, as sometimes happened in later expositions of the "Two Tables" of the Decalogue. The "Golden Rule" (1.2c) could be read as an exposition of "Love your neighbor as yourself," but in what follows loving God and loving neighbor are not separated; in fact all the rules that follow, with the possible exception of idolatry (3.4), have to do with human relations. Nevertheless, the object of all this is "to please God" (cf. 4.12). The interpretive phrase added to the biblical commandment, "You shall love the God *who made you,*" implies the basis for the obligation.

And how does one please God? By not forsaking his commandments (4.13). Notice that the predominant form in the Way of Life is the "commandment," most often in the "apodictic" style found in the Decalogue and some other biblical codes: "You shall (not) . . . ," otherwise in the simple imperative (which also dominates chapters 7–15). Sometimes there is a stated reason or warrant: "Do not be a liar, for lying leads to theft"; but more often not. The commandments stand on their own; one hears and (ideally) obeys.

Whose is the commanding voice that speaks in the *Didache?* The introduction and conclusion to the Way of Life suggest that it is God who commands, and the fact that some of the commandments are taken straight from the Bible, including the Decalogue (ch. 2), reinforces that reading. Yet the form of address "My child," at 3.1, 3, 4, 6; 4.1, is in the style of the sage (like Ben Sira: chapter 3, above) addressing his pupil. Perhaps we are to hear Jesus as this sage; perhaps he is "the Lord" who teaches God's commandments throughout. That is evidently the way the book is construed in the subtitle of the eleventh-century manuscript. The last of the second-century compilers or editors understood the two commandments at the head of the Way of Life as Jesus' commandments (Matt. 22: 37–39 and parallels) and *interpreted* them ("What these maxims teach is this") by composing and inserting here a harmony of sayings of the Lord from various sources, mostly Matthew and Luke (1.3b–6).[10]

Yet Jesus is not named here—or anywhere in the Two Ways part of the *Didache*. Further, there is absolutely no narrative to suggest the identity of the authoritative speaker; how different the *Didache* is in this respect from Matthew!

A number of the commandments are quoted nearly verbatim from the Bible, and there are many other echoes, of varying intensity, of scripture. Yet the various compilers of the *Didache* have treated the biblical verses with remarkable freedom, sometimes setting direct quotations, even of the Decalogue, side by side with interpretive restatements or simply additional commandments, in identical style (see especially ch. 2). The latest redactor used the Gospels of Matthew and Luke with equal freedom, along with other writings that apparently stood in his Bible but not in ours (the *Shepherd of Hermas* and a version of Ben Sira different from the one we know), rearranging, combining, and editing his excerpts for rhetorical effect.[11] The claim is nowhere advanced that the "commandments" are authoritative because they are based on scripture (the nearest thing to such a claim is the formula that introduces the proverb quoted from Ben Sira, literally "it was said"). Indeed, the free quotation and redaction of biblical material counts against the implication of such authority. We are thus in danger of being misled by the modern editors who are careful to mark all biblical allusions in the text; the evidence within the text suggests that the several compilers of the *Didache* and the Christians for whose instruction they wrote did not yet think of "the Bible" as having the same fixity and absoluteness that we are accustomed to attribute to it. The "commandments" listed here are not to be obeyed because they are (some of them) in the Bible, but because they represent the way of "pleasing God."[12]

The ambiguity, whether studied or an accident of the text's history, about the authority behind the commandments leaves the way open for them to be heard at various levels of what we might call Christian sophistication. At the lowest level, there is much here which a simple believer could take as simply rules for keeping in tune with the divine order of things, practices that the Greeks would call *eusebeia* and the Romans *religio*, but that a satirist might call "superstition": being careful of the source of the meat one eats;

using cold water, if possible, for baptism; praying three times a day; being careful to fast not on Mondays and Thursdays but on Wednesdays and Fridays. At a more sophisticated level, all the commandments alike—what we would call the "ritual" as well as the "moral" commandments—are pointers to the unlimited obligation owed to "the God who made you." The sophisticated learner would be pressed also to resolve the ambiguity of "the Lord's" identity, which in the text as it stands blurs Jesus' commands to the church with the commanding voice of God in scripture. The *Didache* offers no "doctrine of the Trinity" to help.

One of the final compilers, perhaps the last, has introduced another theme which now frames the whole collection, and which we may paraphrase, "Try to be perfect." The strongest statement of the theme is in the final chapter: "For the whole time of your faith will be of no use to you unless you are perfected in the last time" (16.2b, trans. Kraft). This statement stands near the beginning of a series of warnings in apocalyptic style, composed of extracts from the "Synoptic Apocalypse," mostly Matthew's version, and a few other texts, which solemnly closes the handbook with an implication of impending Judgment. The way in which this apocalyptic chapter has been composed is strikingly like the interpolated section at the beginning of the Way of Life, 1.3b–6, and may well be by the same "editor." In that composition, too, the theme is sounded: "If someone strikes you on the right cheek, turn to him the other too, *and you will be perfect*" (1.4). Perhaps, originally, a similar phrase stood at the end of the next series: "If someone deprives you of your property, do not ask for it back, *for thus you can be perfect.*"[13] We hear it again at the transition from the Two Ways to the "church order" material, 6.2: "If you can bear the Lord's full yoke, you will be perfect. But if you cannot, then do what you can." Then a specific example: "Now about food: undertake what you can. But keep strictly away from what is offered to idols, for that implies worshiping dead gods" (6.3). The effect of these notes, taken in their sequence in the final version of the *Didache,* is to have undermined the absoluteness of the "perfection" demanded at the end by the concessions that have preceded. The "perfection" demanded by this ethic (which the compiler may have found in Matthew 5:48) is transformed into an ideal to be pursued, according to one's ability. Thus our version of the *Didache* represents the first instance of interpreting Jesus' radical sayings in the Sermon on the Mount in that fashion—an interpretation which would become very popular in modern times. A similar flexibility characterizes the ritual and governance requirements of this document: "If you do not have running water, baptize in some other. If you cannot in cold, then in warm. If you have neither, then pour water on the head three times" (7.2–3). "Before the baptism, moreover, the one who baptizes and the one being baptized must fast, *and any others who can*" (7.4). "In the case of prophets, however, you should let them give thanks in their own way" (10.7; compare also 11.11). "If [the traveler who wants to settle with you] has no trade, *use your own judgment* in taking steps for him to live with you as a Christian without being idle" (12.4; cf. 13.7).

All of this may seem a little bewildering, as a guide to be set before new Christians. Yet we must remember that these are not guidelines for an individual's meditation, but an ethic to be taught and administered within a community. Not only is this made obvious by the fusing of the Two Ways with the rules for conducting worship and treating church leaders, it is presupposed by the *Didache*'s form of the Two Ways and indicated explicitly at 4.1–4:

> My child, day and night "you should remember him who preaches God's word to you," and honor him as you would the Lord. For where the Lord's nature is discussed, there the Lord is. Every day you should seek the company of saints to enjoy their refreshing conversation. You must not start a schism, but reconcile those at strife. "Your judgments must be fair." You must not play favorites when reproving transgressions. You must not be of two minds about your decision.

Note that the catechumen is already being trained to participate in the community's process of mutual admonition and discipline, a process which we found indicated already in Paul's advice to the Thessalonian Christians, and which also reminds us again of an important element in the Rule of the Qumran Essenes.[14] The loose-jointed and multilayered collection of "commandments" comprised by the *Didache* are thus not only the product of the ongoing "conversation" of "the saints," but suited for further use in just such discussion and "judgment." The practice of confession before the assembled group (4.14) reinforces this responsibility of each to the community, and the concluding, eschatological warning recalls the same obligation: "Meet together frequently in your search for what is good for your souls, since a lifetime of faith will be of no advantage to you unless you prove perfect at the very last" (16.2). The perfection required by the *Didache* is not to be found in the commandments abstracted from this communal context—all the concessions and inconsistencies piled up in the collection imply the same point—but only in those regular meetings of brothers and sisters who "search for what is good for [their] souls."

Our Role in God's Drama: Irenaeus

We have been looking at instances of the ways the early Christian movement turned while struggling to develop distinctive and appropriate forms of living. Not all are harmonious with one another, just as the groups that produced them were not always harmonious. Yet several of the texts we have sampled, disparate written deposits of the struggles for a Christian ethos, have become parts of a larger whole, a "New Testament" and a "Bible." Our final sample will show one way—a very influential way, as it turned out—of combining these diverse witnesses into one complex and doctrinal lesson, into a *story*.

In the last decade of the second century, Irenaeus the bishop of Lyons wrote for a friend Marcianus, probably a priest, a little summary of Christian belief, which he called *Proof* [or *Demonstration*] of the Apostolic Preaching. It will serve well as our final sample of second-century Christian moral writing, for Irenaeus was not a strikingly original thinker. Rather, he undertook to articulate the "catholic" consensus, that is, the single faith which the church had received, as he believed, "from the apostles and their disciples," and preached, "although scattered throughout the whole world," yet "with perfect harmony, as if she possessed only one mouth" (*Against Heresies* 1.10.1–3)[15] Irenaeus was aware, of course, that there was in fact a cacophony of different voices claiming to represent the true Christian faith, but he was convinced that the dissonance was the result of outside influences and the ambition of a series of individual teachers. When he wrote to Marcianus, he had recently completed a five-volume work against such people, which he called *The Exposé and Overthrow of What Is Falsely Called "Gnosis"* (from which come the words just quoted). Irenaeus still had the "Gnostics" and other heretics very much in mind as he wrote the *Proof,* but this book is not primarily antiheretical. Rather, it wants to exhibit and confirm what the catholic tradition says, "that you may preserve your faith entire and so be pleasing to God who made you" (*Proof* 1, Robinson).[16]

The last phrase quoted is itself traditional. We recognize it from the beginning of the Two Ways, *Didache* 1.2a = *Barnabas* 19.2a. Further, Irenaeus follows it with a free variation of the Two Ways figure:

> For the road of all those who see is a single upward path, lit by heavenly light; but the ways of those who see not are many and dark and divergent. The former road leads to the kingdom of heaven by

uniting man with God, but the others bring down to death by severing man from God.

New here are the notion that salvation consists in the union of believers with God, a central theme in Irenaeus' own theology, and the contrast between the "single path" of the Catholics and the multiple schisms of the heretics.

How does one "please God" and thus stay on the single path that leads to union with him? In the *Didache* this seemed a simple matter of following the guidelines suggested by the "commandments," but Irenaeus is more sophisticated. Because "man is an animal made up of soul and body, . . . there is both bodily holiness, the safeguard of abstinence from all shameful things and all wicked deeds, and holiness of soul, the preservation in its integrity of faith in God" (2). He is more explicit a paragraph later: "We must keep strictly, without deviation, the rule of faith, and carry out the commands of God" (3). The "rule (Greek *kanōn*) of faith" or "of truth" (cf. *Against Heresies* 1.1.20) is, at its simplest, the creed recited at baptism, which Irenaeus rehearses or paraphrases several times in the *Proof* (e.g., 3, 6, 40). As we see the use that Irenaeus has made of this "rule" throughout the *Proof,* however, we realize that it is for him far more than a list of propositions to which one must assent. It is rather a kind of plot summary of the story of God's purposes and actions for humanity, a key by which one is able to read the Bible in such a way as to flesh out that plot and in turn to use the Bible, thus read, to interpret one's life.

Faith and morality are for Irenaeus as inseparable as soul and body; it was doubtless in his struggle against the Gnostics, with their exaltation of "spirit" and contempt for the body, that Irenaeus concluded that the whole Jewish and Christian tradition taught that soul and body alike are objects of God's creation and salvation. Therefore faith entails care for all our embodied relationships, and affects them. In his own words:

> Action, then, is preserved by faith, because "unless you believe," says Isaias, "you shall not continue"; and faith is given by truth, since faith rests upon reality: for we shall believe what really is, as it is, and, believing what really is, as it is for ever, keep a firm hold on our assent to it. (*Proof* 3)

That is not very far from the way a modern anthropologist, Clifford Geertz, would describe the same matter: our world view—our culturally or subculturally taught picture of "what really is"—must somehow correspond to our ethos—the normative pattern of our "action"; that correspondence is represented and guaranteed to us by our sacred symbols.[17]

The "sacred symbols" for Irenaeus are to be found, in a nutshell, in the "Rule of Faith." But that, in turn, points to the Bible as a book full of symbols. Yes, when we come to Irenaeus we can speak of "the Bible," as we found we could not yet in the case of the *Didache*. As the late Cyril Richardson remarked, "he is the first Christian writer who worked with the New Testament much as we do. It is for him as for us part of the Bible, although he does not put it exactly that way."[18] An overstatement, perhaps, for apart from his insistence on the "Fourfold Gospel" it is not clear that Irenaeus thought of a fixed canon of the other authoritative Christian writings; yet with that qualification the statement stands. Space does not permit a full discussion of Irenaeus' use of scripture, but there are certain patterns which appear in his exposition that are particularly revealing. They show how the Christian perception of the way things really are, for Irenaeus, give shape and meaning to Christian action. A brief outline of these patterns will furnish a fitting conclusion to our sampling of Christian moral grammar, for in them Irenaeus draws together the characteristic modes of reading scripture that had developed by his time, and his own synthesis points to the way in which the main stream of Christian interpretation would flow for subsequent centuries, until the modern era.[19]

For convenience and clarity, we can divide Irenaeus' interpretive strategies into four—not to say that he would have distinguished them in this way, or that they are always separable. (1) Some things said in scripture are figures or analogies of other things: later events, concepts, structures of the natural world, and so on. (2) Sometimes the speaker or actor in an Old Testament passage is Christ, or rather, the pre-incarnate Word of God. (3) Prophecies often have a double meaning, one for their own time and a more significant one pointing ahead to the time of Jesus and the church. (4) The whole Bible, which for Irenaeus already, like ours, ran from Genesis to Revelation (though perhaps it included some books, like *Enoch*, that ours does not, and may have lacked a few that are in our New Testament), tells one continuous story. An example or two will show how each strategy works.

Chapter 32 of the *Proof* provides a good example of Irenaeus' figural reading, though it violates all our notions of the right way to read a text. The "dust" from which God made the first human, according to Genesis 2:7, was from virgin soil—since the text also says that it had not yet rained and there was no one to till the ground (v. 5). Thus the first man was made by the union of God's will and wisdom with a "virgin"—and so was Christ. Irenaeus then transfers the "virgin" figure to Eve, to elaborate the analogy: "And just as it was through a virgin who disobeyed that man was stricken and fell and died, so too it was through the Virgin, who obeyed the word of God, that man resuscitated by life received life." "For," he continues, "Adam had necessarily to be restored in Christ, that mortality be absorbed in immortality, and Eve in Mary, that a virgin, become the advocate of a virgin, should undo and destroy virginal disobedience by virginal obedience" (33).

The correspondence between Adam and Christ, between creation and redemption, is of central importance for Irenaeus' own theology. He was fascinated by a line in the opening doxology of the Letter to the Ephesians, which the Revised Standard Version translates like this: "For he has made known to us in all wisdom and insight the mystery of his will, according to his purpose which he set forth in Christ as a plan for the fullness of time, to unite all things in him, things in heaven and things on earth" (Eph 1:9–10). Irenaeus repeatedly uses the verb translated here "to unite" (often translated "recapitulate," from the Latin equivalent of the Greek verb) and its corresponding noun to refer to the Incarnation's "summing up" the course of created and fallen humanity's life and "restoring" or "reestablishing" it into the pattern intended by God. The notion is not completely original with him, however. He found the correspondence between Adam and Christ in Paul's Letter to the Romans (Rom. 5:12–21; cf. 1 Cor. 15:44–49), and Justin Martyr had worked out part of the parallel Irenaeus uses. Moreover, the concept that God would at the end of days remake the world to fit the pattern of the original, good creation is an important element in Jewish as well as Christian apocalyptic thought.

Chapter 9 contains a different kind of figuration. Each of the seven "forms of service" (Robinson) given by the Spirit to the one on whom it rests, according to Isaiah 11:2–3, corresponds to one of the seven heavens (concentric planetary orbits or spheres) which, Irenaeus assumed everyone knows, surround the earth. Here the scriptural text does not *pre*figure a subsequent event (rather, it speaks directly of the incarnate Son of God by prophecy), but figures an aspect of the structure of the world itself. It might be better to put it the other way round: the way the world is made, according to the up-to-date astronomy Irenaeus followed, figures the character of the Son of God, once scripture gives us the key. By calling the gifts enumerated by Isaiah "forms of service" (his Greek word was apparently *diakoniai*), Irenaeus reveals that he is also thinking of Paul's list in 1 Corinthians 12:4–11, but he does not mention the latter passage; Paul had unfortunately listed more than seven gifts there.

Irenaeus is not just playing idly with numbers here or elsewhere, as for example when he insists that there must be four Gospels and no more, because there are four cardinal directions, four winds, and four Living Creatures around the throne of God (Ezek. 1; Rev. 4:6–8; *Against Heresies* 3.11.8). Anyone who has considered Pythagoras' theory of numbers, or read Philo's use of the Pythagorean numbers to interpret verses of the Pentateuch, will know that educated people could take such numerical coincidences as serious clues to correspondences in the meaningful universe. We might say that, for Irenaeus, there is a pattern in "nature," in "history," and in the mind of God; that pattern is coherent; and faithful reading of the Bible can discover it. Of course he is also tacitly refuting the Gnostics, for whom the seven planetary spheres are hostile sentry-posts in the prison, namely this world, in which the gnostic spirits are trapped until they are enlightened and freed. Not so, says Irenaeus: the whole glorious universe hiddenly reflects the good purpose of God and awaits the "summing up" or "restoration" accomplished by the incarnate Word. What has that belief to do with behavior? This symbolically coherent universe is "what really is" (cf. *Proof* 3); Gnostic contempt for the created order, like Gnostic contempt for the body (cf. 2), is contrary to the reality that faith discerns.

The second category of Irenaeus' readings is simpler, if just as remote from our way of thinking. For example, in chapter 44 he takes up the curious story found in Genesis 18–19, which for any careful reader presents problems. The opening sentence tells us that "the Lord appeared" to Abraham, yet the next continues that "three men stood in front of him." In the dialogue that ensues between Abraham and these three, their side is represented sometimes by "they said," sometimes, "he said," or again, "the LORD said." And at 18:33 we are told, "the LORD went his way," while at 19:1, "the *two* angels came to Sodom." No wonder Irenaeus concludes that "Two, then, of the three, were angels, but one the Son of God," and that the two occurrences of the word "LORD" in Genesis 19:24 refer respectively to the Son and the Father. Justin had already worked out this reading of the text, and in many other passages as well he was able to find the Word, that is, what later Christians would call "the second person of the Trinity," speaking or acting. So Irenaeus finds the Son of God, rather than angels, on Jacob's ladder (which also figures the cross, thus an example of our first way of reading) (45), and speaking from Moses' burning bush (46).

The third category is also straightforward and altogether familiar in Christian argument from the beginnings of the movement:

> That all these things would come to pass was foretold by the Spirit of God through the prophets, that those who served God in truth might believe firmly in them; for what was quite impossible to our nature, and therefore like to be little believed in by men, God caused to be announced in advance by the prophets, that from the prediction made long beforehand, when at last the event took place just as had been foretold, we might know that it was God, who had revealed to us in advance our redemption. (42)

The final category is more innovative. Although one could say that all the ingredients for it were present already, Irenaeus seems to be the first author, of those whose works survive, to articulate the notion that the whole of humankind and of the world has one history, which is told in the biblical narrative. This history Irenaeus outlines in chapters 4 through 30 of the *Proof,* though he adds elements elsewhere. Its beginning point is the creation of the world and the primal innocence and subsequent disobedience of the first human couple, as told in Genesis. Its climax is the incarnation of the Word and Son of God; its denouement his coming again to judge all (85). Each of these major "acts" of the drama had been part of Christian belief since the first century; as we saw above, the correspondence of Adam with Christ was introduced already by Paul. What is new about Irenaeus' exposition, however, is that he systematically fills in the narrative between Creation-and-Fall and the account of Jesus' appearance by following the biblical narrative—especially the narratives of the Pentateuch, but also parts at least of the subsequent account of Israel's history. Thus Israel's history, construed in the prophetic (and deuteronomic) perspective of sin and redemption, is subsumed into what has emerged by Irenaeus' time as the universal history of God's plan for human redemption, in which a "new people" replaces Israel (86–87, 91–94), but in which Israel had a necessary and instructive part. Again, the "figural" or "typological" reading of the Bible had implied many if not most of the parts of this way of understanding Christianity's antecedents (see, for example, the scriptural "proofs" in the *Epistle of Barnabas*), yet the dramatic plot as a whole had not previously (as far as we know) been worked out. Yet its power, once stated, can be sensed by the extent to which, even now, it seems to us a natural way to read the Bible. From the ever so much more elaborate exposition of these themes in Augustine's *City of God,* through the medieval cycles of miracle plays and narrative sequences in stained glass, through Milton and a large part of the corpus of modern literature, to twentieth-century "biblical theology," the Christian Bible, beginning with Genesis and ending with Apocalypse, is construed as a single, complex drama.

It is a story, Irenaeus claims, in which each of us is a character. The difficulties we face are explained by that great struggle between God's will for our redemption and the Satan-inspired outworkings of disobedience which provides the dramatic tension of the plot; our hope is made possible by our union with the Son, the Image of God, who came to "recapitulate" that struggle, to overcome it in his victory, and to "restore" our nature; our future is resurrection to face his judgment and reward. That is the subtle pattern within which each of our actions must be deemed good or bad. As Irenaeus himself summed it up:

> This, beloved, is the preaching of the truth, and this is the manner of our salvation, and this is the way of life, announced by the prophets and ratified by Christ and handed over by the apostles and handed down by the Church in the whole world to her children. This must be kept in all security, with good will, and by being well-pleasing to God through good works and sound moral character. (*Proof* 98)

Afterword

Out of his treasure, wrote Matthew, the Christian scribe brought things old and things new. In the Christian movement were woven together the great traditions of the past—of Greece and Rome and Israel—and the traditions of the little communities in Galilee and Judea and all around the Mediterranean basin. And these traditions were amalgamated with and transformed by "news," "gospel," novel claims, novel experiences, interpretations that skewed the traditions and sometimes stood them on their heads.

Those of us who want most to follow in the way of the first Christians tend to focus our attention on what was new about them. What was unique about their morality? What was the essence of their ethics? I have argued throughout this book that these questions do not represent an adequate way toward understanding. To obtain the essence of something, we have to boil it down, distill, filter out; what is left is not the living thing, but a residue, an abstraction.

In the second century it was the sophisticated detractors of Christianity who emphasized its newness. "Novel," wrote Tacitus, and therefore, "a superstition." Christianity's defenders insisted that it was not new at all, but as old as creation, as old as the sacred books of the Jews, its ideas familiar in the best of the Greek and Roman philosophers, its practices not dissimilar from the best of pagan ritual and life. Yet, in other contexts, they also could emphasize its differences and its novelty. In order to understand the first Christians, it is not enough either to abstract their novelties or to add up the "parallels" and "influences" from their environment. It is the patterns of the whole that we have been trying to discern.

We cannot ever fully know the world of the early Christians; still less can we re-create it. To be sure, those movements in the history of Christendom which have sought to restore the church to its "primitive" purity, from the Montanists to the Campbellites, have released powerful currents of change. Yet what they in fact brought about was inevitably something unlike the past. There is no time machine. We must live in our own world, which is irreversibly different from that of the first Christians.

Nevertheless, we have things to learn from what we can see of their world. For one thing, we can learn that ours is not the only possible conception of the way things are and must be. Even as there are things about the world of the first Christians which are impossible for us, there are other things which may nag and tear at the edges of our own world, making it seem perhaps not so inevitable, not so simply factual as we thought.

In the first generations of Christians, moreover, we see many people who have a kind of double vision. Two different kinds of symbolized universe overlap in their minds and in their social experience. On the one hand there is the world so commonplace that no one in everyday life would think of speaking of it as "symbols." It was simply there, for them and their neighbors, as ours is for us. On the other hand there is the strange new world of the creating, caring, and judging God, of the crucified Messiah raised from the dead. There are the little groups of fellow believers, of brothers and sisters, children of God, with their simple but powerful rituals, their vigorous admonitions of one another, their moments of high emotion, sometimes trances, ecstasy, experiences of the Spirit—in these meetings this other world seems more vivid than the ordinary one. Yet somehow they had to live in both, and it was not easy to find the way to do that. There were many disagreements, many alternative ways, some of which failed. From them everyone who craves a vision of a juster, kinder world, everyone caught not merely between what is and what ought to be, but between conflicting certainties, disparate but impinging maps of what *is,* all may have something to learn.

Notes

Introduction

1. The phrase is James M. Gustafson's ("The Church: A Community of Moral Discourse," *The Church as Moral Decision-Maker* [Philadelphia: Pilgrim Press, 1970], pp. 83–95), employed to good effect recently by Allen Verhey, *The Great Reversal: Ethics and the New Testament* (Grand Rapids: Wm. B. Eerdmans Publishing Co., 1984).

2. Stanley Hauerwas, *A Community of Character: Toward a Constructive Christian Social Ethic* (Notre Dame and London: University of Notre Dame Press, 1981).

3. The classic discussion of this process of socialization and world formation is Peter L. Berger and Thomas Luckmann, *The Social Construction of Reality: A Treatise in the Sociology of Knowledge* (Garden City, N.Y.: Doubleday & Co., 1966).

4. Clifford Geertz, "Ethos, World View, and the Analysis of Sacred Symbols," in *The Interpretation of Cultures* (New York: Basic Books, 1973), pp. 126–141 (originally published in *The Antioch Review* in 1957). The quotations that follow are taken from p. 127.

Chapter 1: The Social Setting

1. For further discussion of the life and institutions of the polis, see John E. Stambaugh and David L. Balch, *The New Testament in Its Social Environment* (Philadelphia: Westminster Press, 1986), ch. 6.

2. Translation of *Antigone* by Elizabeth Wyckoff, in *Sophocles I,* ed. David Grene and Richmond Lattimore (*The Complete Greek Tragedies;* Chicago and London: University of Chicago Press, 1954). On *Antigone* as conflict between clan rights and polis, see Werner Jaeger, *Paideia: The Ideals of Greek Culture,* 3 vols. (New York and Oxford: Oxford University Press, 1943–45),

vol. 1 (2nd ed. 1945), p. 282, and Alasdair MacIntyre, *After Virtue: A Study in Moral Theory* (Notre Dame: University of Notre Dame Press, 1981), p. 135. On the "urbanity" of Sophocles, see Jaeger, *Paideia*, vol. 1, pp. 271–284.

3. Text and English translation in Herbert Musurillo, *The Acts of the Christian Martyrs* (Oxford: Clarendon Press, 1972), pp. 106–131. I have departed from Musurillo's translation of 5.5 above.

4. A small excerpt from a long list in P.Oxy. 1380, adapted from a translation by Ramsay MacMullen.

5. Trans. by H. Lamar Crosby, Loeb Classical Library.

6. Philo tells the story himself in his two treatises, *Flaccus* and *Embassy to Gaius*. See also Josephus, *Antiquities* 18.257–309.

7. Jaeger, *Paideia*, vol. 2, p. 54.

8. The story was reported by a second-century Greek writer, Antisthenes, and preserved in fragments of the *Mirabilia* by Phlegon: Felix Jacoby, *Die Fragmente der griechischen Historiker*, vol. IIB (Berlin: Weidmann, 1929), No. 257, F36(III) (pp. 1169–1185).

9. Trans. by G. Buchanan Gray in R. H. Charles, ed., *The Apocrypha and Pseudepigrapha of the Old Testament*, vol. 2 (Oxford: Clarendon Press, 1913, repr. 1963), p. 631.

10. Geza Vermes, *The Dead Sea Scrolls in English* (Harmondsworth and Baltimore: Penguin Books, 1962), p. 138.

11. Carneades' arguments were reconstructed from the fragments of Cicero's *Republic*, book 3, and elsewhere, and set within the history of debate on the topic by Wilhelm Capelle, "Griechische Ethik und römischer Imperialismus," *Klio* 25 (1932), 86–113.

12. *Orations* 26.94, trans. by James H. Oliver in "The Ruling Power: A Study of the Roman Empire in the Second Century After Christ Through the Roman Oration of Aelius Aristides," *TAPS*, n.s. 43/4 (1953), 905.

13. Josephus, *Antiquities* 14.223–227, 234, 235, 241–246.

14. We know of the event from the speech of Flaccus' defense lawyer: Cicero, *Pro Flacco* 66–69. See the brief discussion in E. Mary Smallwood, *The Jews Under Roman Rule from Pompey to Diocletian* (Leiden: E. J. Brill, 1976), pp. 126–127.

15. *Orations* 26.39, trans. by Oliver, p. 899.

16. I have adapted these categories from a recent article by Karl Christ, "Grundfragen der römischen Sozialstruktur," in *Studien zur antiken Sozialgeschichte: Festschrift für Friedrich Vittinghoff*, ed. by Werner Eck, Hartmut Gal

sterer, and Hartmut Wolff (Kölner historische Abhandlungen, 28; Cologne: Böhlau, 1980), pp. 197–228. For more discussion of social status in the environment of early Christianity, see Stambaugh and Balch (see note 1 of this chapter).

17. Friedrich Vittinghoff, "Soziale Struktur and politisches System der hohen römischen Kaiserzeit," *Historische Zeitschrift* 230 (1980), 30–55.

18. The first quotation is from P.Oxy. 2852, ed. and trans. by R. F. Tannenbaum and P. A. M. Seuren, in *The Oxyrhynchus Papyri*, vol. 38, ed. by Gerald M. Browne et al. (London: British Academy, 1971), pp. 64–67. Lusanias' query, addressed to the oracle at Dodona, is quoted by H. S. Versnel, "Religious Mentality in Ancient Prayer," in H. S. Versnel (ed.), *Faith, Hope, and Worship: Aspects of Religious Mentality in the Ancient World* (Studies in Greek and Roman Religion, 2; Leiden: E. J. Brill, 1981), p. 25. The last quotation is from *Ps. Sol.* 17.23, trans. by G. Buchanan Gray (see above, n. 9).

19. Epictetus, *Discourses* 3.22.5–8, trans. by W. A. Oldfather, Loeb Classical Library.

20. Trans. by H. Rackham (Loeb), emphasis added.

Chapter 2: The Great Traditions: Greece and Rome

1. Robert Redfield, *The Little Community: Viewpoints for the Study of a Human Whole* (Comparative Studies of Cultures and Civilizations; Chicago: University of Chicago Press, 1955), p. 3.

2. Pseudo-Plutarch, *The Education of Children* 10 = *Moralia* 7D, my trans.

3. Ibid., *Moralia* 7E, trans. by Frank Cole Babbitt (Loeb).

4. See, for example, John Dillon, *The Middle Platonists 80 B.C. to A.D. 220* (Ithaca: Cornell University Press, 1977), pp. 184–230. For further study of the Platonic school in Roman times this book is an excellent starting point.

5. Plutarch, *The E at Delphi* 17–21 = *Moralia* 392A–394C, my trans.

6. Trans. by Phillip H. de Lacy and Benedict Einarson (Loeb).

7. Trans. by W. C. Helmbold (Loeb).

8. A. D. Nock, *Conversion: The Old and the New in Religion from Alexander the Great to Augustine of Hippo* (Oxford: Oxford University Press, 1933), ch. 11.

9. Trans. by W. C. Helmbold (Loeb).

10. Trans. by Frank Cole Babbitt (Loeb).

11. There is only one complete English translation of the extant works, and that, printed with the Greek text from Hense's edition, is by Cora E.

Lutz, *Musonius Rufus: "The Roman Socrates"* (Yale Classical Studies, 10; New Haven: Yale University Press, 1947). I have used Lutz's translation except where otherwise indicated.

12. This is from a passage that Epictetus quoted from his teacher in a lost work *On Friendship,* which in turn was excerpted by the anthologist Stobaeus. It is Fragment 38 in Lutz, from whose translation I have quoted, and Fragment 4 in the Loeb edition of Epictetus, ed. by W. A. Oldfather.

13. This is a complex and debated issue. See the careful discussion by I. G. Kidd, "Stoic Intermediates and the End for Man," in A. A. Long, ed., *Problems in Stoicism* (London: Athlone Press, 1971), pp. 150–172.

14. These are now conveniently available in Abraham J. Malherbe, ed., *The Cynic Epistles: A Study Edition* (SBL Sources for Biblical Study, 12; Missoula, Mont.: Scholars Press, 1977), containing a Greek text and translation by several of Malherbe's students. I cite from this edition by the attributed author and the number assigned the epistle (e.g., Diogenes 2), with the page and line number where needed.

15. A great many *chriai,* as such anecdotes were called, were collected by Diogenes Laertius in the third century A.D., in book 6 of his *Lives of Eminent Philosophers,* readily available in the Loeb Classical Library.

16. Diogenes Laertius 6.57, 58, 46, 38; cf. Diogenes 35.2–3; 33; Malherbe, *The Cynic Epistles,* pp. 147, 140–143.

17. Abraham J. Malherbe, building on earlier work by G. A. Gerhard, has shown that the sources, especially the Cynic epistles, reveal a distinction made in antiquity between "harsh" and "mild" Cynics; I am dependent on his work for most of what is said here about them. See his article "Cynics," *Interpreter's Dictionary of the Bible,* Supplementary Volume (Nashville: Abingdon Press, 1976), pp. 201–203, and "Self-Definition Among Epicureans and Cynics," in Ben F. Meyer and E. P. Sanders, eds., *Jewish and Christian Self-Definition,* Vol. 3: *Self-Definition in the Greco-Roman World* (Philadelphia: Fortress Press, 1982), pp. 46–59.

18. These can all be found conveniently, with an English translation and commentary, in Cyril Bailey, *Epicurus: The Extant Remains* (Oxford: Clarendon Press, 1926; reprinted Hildesheim and New York: Georg Olms, 1970). I have used Bailey's translation in what follows, except where otherwise noted.

19. For Epicurean sculpture and other forms of Epicurean "recruitment," see the fascinating book by Bernard Frischer, *The Sculpted Word: Epicureanism and Philosophical Recruitment in Ancient Greece* (Berkeley, Los Angeles, London: University of California Press, 1982), which was called to my attention by my colleague Abraham Malherbe.

20. Pseudo-Plutarch, *The Education of Children* 11 = *Moralia* 8E–F, acknowledges that poor people will not be able to afford the kind of education

he recommends, but insists that they should blame luck, not him. In any case, they must do the best they can. Among the Cynics, some insisted that it was possible to philosophize even while earning a living as an artisan; Simon the shoemaker, supposed to have been a friend of Socrates, was portrayed as the model: see Ronald F. Hock, "Simon the Shoemaker as an Ideal Cynic," *GRBS* 17 (1976), 41–53.

21. For a brief introduction, see John E. Stambaugh and David L. Balch, *The New Testament in Its Social Environment* (Philadelphia: Westminster Press, 1986), pp. 121–122; see further Henri Marrou, *A History of Education in Antiquity* (New York: Sheed & Ward, 1956).

22. See Sarah B. Pomeroy, *Goddesses, Whores, Wives, and Slaves: Women in Classical Antiquity* (New York: Schocken Books, 1975), p. 170.

23. Dio Chrysostom, *Orations* 32.8–12; quotation from para. 8, trans. by H. Lamar Crosby (Loeb, 3:179).

Chapter 3: The Great Traditions: Israel

1. See 1 and 2 Maccabees. For brief accounts of the cultural context and effects of the revolt, see Elias Bickerman, *From Ezra to the Last of the Maccabees* (New York: Schocken Books, 1962); Martin Hengel, *Jews, Greeks, and Barbarians* (Philadelphia: Fortress Press, 1980). For more extensive treatments, see Elias Bickerman, *The God of the Maccabees: Studies on the Meanings and Origin of the Maccabean Revolt* (Studies in Judaism in Late Antiquity, 32; Leiden: E. J. Brill, 1979); Martin Hengel, *Judaism and Hellenism* (London: SCM Press; Philadelphia: Fortress Press, 1974); Victor Tcherikover, *Hellenistic Civilization and the Jews* (Philadelphia: Jewish Publication Society, 1959).

2. *On Rewards and Punishments* 117, trans. by F. H. Colson (Loeb).

3. See above, chapter 1. For a detailed survey of Israel's relationship with Rome, see E. Mary Smallwood, *The Jews Under Roman Rule from Pompey to Diocletian: A Study in Political Relations* (2nd ed., Leiden: E. J. Brill, 1981). On the ways in which Jews of the Diaspora perceived their identity, as revealed in many small and fragmentary examples of their writings, excluding the great corpus of Philo's works, see John J. Collins, *Between Athens and Jerusalem: Jewish Identity in the Hellenistic Diaspora* (New York: Crossroad Publishing Co., 1983).

4. The Greek version of Ben Sira became very popular with Christians and eventually was incorporated into the "deuterocanonical" part of the Christian Bible or, in Protestant Bibles, the Apocrypha. There it is known as Ecclesiasticus or, from the Greek rendering of Yeshua's patronymic, Sirach. Although the book ultimately was excluded from the Hebrew Bible, it was discussed and sometimes quoted in Talmud and midrash. Fragmentary copies of the Hebrew text found at Qumran and Masada attest to its use by various groups in the first century, and parts of several copies found

in the storeroom of an ancient synagogue in Cairo show that it was still popular in the Middle Ages. All quotations here are from the RSV unless otherwise noted.

5. Aristeas is conveniently available in R. H. Charles, ed., *The Apocrypha and Pseudepigrapha of the Old Testament*, vol. 2 (Oxford: Clarendon Press, 1913, repr. 1963), pp. 83–122.

6. See A. R. Hands, *Charities and Social Aid in Greece and Rome* (Aspects of Greek and Roman Life; Ithaca, N.Y.: Cornell University Press, 1968), esp. pp. 62–88.

7. Hans Conzelmann, "Die Mutter der Weisheit," in Erich Dinkler, ed., *Zeit und Geschichte; Dankesgabe an Rudolf Bultmann zum 80. Geburtstag* (Tübingen: J. C. B. Mohr [Paul Siebeck], 1964), pp. 225–234.

8. See Martin Hengel, *Judaism and Hellenism*, vol. 1, pp. 131–162.

9. Translations of the Dead Sea Scrolls, unless otherwise indicated, are from Geza Vermes, *The Dead Sea Scrolls in English* (2nd ed.; Baltimore and Harmondsworth: Penguin Books, 1975). I have occasionally altered his captialization. Also I use the standard abbreviations rather than those of Vermes, and line as well as column numbers (not included in Vermes) so that the reader may find the passages in other editions or in publications of the Hebrew texts: "CD"=Cairo manuscripts of the Damascus Covenant; 1QS=the Community Rule from Cave 1, Qumran; etc.

10. The works of Philo, except for a few of the smaller fragments, are now readily available, with English translation, in 12 volumes of the Loeb Classical Library. Unless otherwise noted, I have used the Loeb translations, by F. H. Colson (vols. 1–10), G. H. Whitaker (1–6), and Ralph Marcus (*QG* and *QE*).

11. See Erwin R. Goodenough, *An Introduction to Philo Judaeus* (2nd ed.; Oxford: Basil Blackwell, 1962), pp. 112–118.

12. For what follows I am largely dependent upon the work of Jacob Neusner and his students. Especially important is their multivolume history of Mishnaic law, culminating in Neusner's *Judaism: The Evidence of the Mishnah* (Chicago and London: University of Chicago Press, 1981).

13. The most widely available translation, and one that is very reliable, is Herbert Danby, *The Mishnah, translated from the Hebrew with Introduction and Brief Explanatory Notes* (London: Oxford University Press, 1933; often reprinted). Unless otherwise noted, quotations are from that translation. Conventionally, references to the Mishnah cite the sections or "tractates" by abbreviated titles (preceded by "m." if there is danger of confusion with other Rabbinic documents) followed by the number of the chapter (or "mishnah") and paragraph. Thus, m.*Berakoth* 2.5 means: tractate *Berakoth* [found in the first division of the Mishnah], chapter 2, paragraph 5.

14. Neusner, *Judaism*, p. 154.

15. Translated by Jacob Neusner, *A History of the Mishnaic Law of Purities*, Part 1 (Studies in Judaism in Late Antiquity; Leiden: E. J. Brill, 1974), p. 46.

16. Ibid., pp. 55f., with small alterations.

17. Neusner, *Judaism*, p. 235.

18. *Antiquities* 1.14, trans. by H. St. J. Thackeray in the Loeb edition.

19. Harold W. Attridge, *The Interpretation of Biblical History in the Antiquitates Judaicae of Flavius Josephus* (Harvard Dissertations in Religion, 7; Missoula, Mont.: Scholars Press, 1976), pp. 38–57.

20. The problem of "monotheism" in Greco-Roman culture is a complicated one; see Robert M. Grant, *Gods and the One God* (Library of Early Christianity; Philadelphia: Westminster Press, 1986).

21. *Against Apion* 1.38, 40, trans. by Thackeray in the Loeb ed.

22. For further discussion of the development of the canon and of different modes of interpretation, see the first part of James Kugel and Rowan A. Greer, *Early Biblical Interpretation* (Library of Early Christianity; Philadelphia: Westminster Press, 1986).

23. Josephus, *Antiquities* 14.185–267.

24. For one strong attack on the problem, see E. P. Sanders, *Paul and Palestinian Judaism* (London: SCM Press; Philadelphia: Fortress Press, 1977).

25. I owe this suggestion to my colleague Robert Wilson.

Chapter 4: The Christian Communities

1. Peter Berger, "The Sociological Study of Sectarianism," *Social Research* 21 (1954), 479, observed: "The attitude toward the world largely determines the inner social structure of the sect." Bryan R. Wilson, *Magic and the Millennium: A Sociological Study of Religious Movements of Protest Among Tribal and Third-World Peoples* (New York: Harper & Row, 1973), classifies different types of sect in terms of their "response to the world" (p. 21).

2. Albert Schweitzer, *The Mystery of the Kingdom of God: The Secret of Jesus' Messiahship and Passion*, trans. by Walter Lowrie (New York: Schocken Books, 1964), esp. ch. 3.

3. The term "socioecology" was coined by Gerd Theissen, on whose analysis much of what follows depends, although I differ with his interpretation on a couple of key points. See his *Sociology of Early Palestinian Christianity* (Philadelphia: Fortress Press, 1978). See also John E. Stambaugh and David

L. Balch, *The New Testament in Its Social Environment* (Philadelphia: Westminster Press, 1986), ch. 4.

4. Trans. by Thomas O. Lambdin in James M. Robinson, ed., *The Nag Hammadi Library in English* (Leiden: E. J. Brill; San Francisco: Harper & Row, 1977). The *Gospel of Thomas* was probably written, in Greek, sometime in the second century, and may contain much earlier traditions. We have fragments of the Greek, and a complete copy in Coptic, made in the fourth century.

5. See Reuven Kimelman, "*Birkat Ha-Minim* and the Lack of Evidence for an Anti-Christian Jewish Prayer in Late Antiquity," in E. P. Sanders, ed., *Jewish and Christian Self-Definition,* vol. 2: *Aspects of Judaism in the Graeco-Roman Period* (Philadelphia: Fortress Press; London: SCM Press, 1981), pp. 226–244.

6. *Inscriptiones Graecae ad Res Romanas Pertinentes* (1906–), 4:1327.

7. Franciszek Sokolowski, *Lois sacrées de l'Asie Mineure* (Ecole Française d'Athènes: Travaux et Memoires . . . , 9; Paris: Boccard, 1955), No. 20; my trans.

8. For a full exposition of 1 Thessalonians from this perspective, see the forthcoming Anchor Bible volume on the Thessalonian letters by Abraham J. Malherbe. See also the first part of chapter 5, below.

9. For a discussion of this precept and the different applications of it in the two letters, see O. Larry Yarbrough, *"Not Like the Gentiles": Marriage Rules in the Letters of Paul* (SBL Dissertation Series, 80; Atlanta: Scholars Press, 1985).

10. The most extensive collection of noncanonical sayings of Jesus published so far, gleaned from ancient literature, will be available soon in the SBL Sources for Biblical Study series (Scholars Press), edited by William Stroker.

11. Trans. by Cyril C. Richardson, *Early Christian Fathers* (Library of Christian Classics; Philadelphia: Westminster Press, 1953).

12. See Luke T. Johnson, "The Use of Leviticus 19 in the Letter of James," *JBL* 101 (1982), 391–401; P. W. van der Horst, *The Sentences of Pseudo-Phocylides* (Studia in Veteris Testamenti Pseudepigrapha, 4; Leiden: E. J. Brill, 1978), pp. 66–67.

13. Trans. by A. M. Harmon, *Lucian, with an English Translation,* vol. 5 (Loeb Classical Library; London: Heinemann; Cambridge, Mass.: Harvard University Press, 1972).

Chapter 5: The Grammar of Early Christian Morals

1. For examples of parenesis, see Abraham J. Malherbe, *Moral Exhortation: A Greco-Roman Sourcebook* (Library of Early Christianity; Philadelphia: Westminster Press, 1986). For a discussion of parenetic letters and examples from antiquity, see Stanley K. Stowers, *Letter Writing in Greco-Roman Antiquity* (Library of Early Christianity; Philadelphia: Westminster Press, 1986).

2. See Malherbe, *Moral Exhortation*, ch. 3, and Stowers, *Letter Writing*, ch. 2.

3. For a discussion of the Gospels as Hellenistic biographies, see David E. Aune, *The New Testament in Its Literary Environment* (Library of Early Christianity; Philadelphia: Westminster Press, forthcoming).

4. For a discussion of the use of epitomes in Greco-Roman exhortation and for pagan examples, see Malherbe, ch. 4, and Hans Dieter Betz, *Essays on the Sermon on the Mount* (Philadelphia: Fortress Press, 1985), pp. 1–16.

5. For anger, see 1QS 5.25–26; for oaths: Josephus, *Jewish War* 2.135; *Antiquities* 15.371.

6. See John P. Meier, *The Vision of Matthew: Christ, Church and Morality in the First Gospel* (Theological Inquiries; New York, Ramsey, N.J., and Toronto: Paulist Press, 1979), pp. 45–51.

7. See above, chapter 4. On Matthew's resistance to the itinerants' ethic, see Leander E. Keck, "Ethics in the Gospel According to Matthew," *Iliff Review* 40/4 (Winter 1984), 39–56, an article that suggested several of the ideas developed below.

8. Unless otherwise noted in what follows, I use the superb translation by Cyril C. Richardson in the volume edited by him, *Early Christian Fathers* (Library of Christian Classics; Philadelphia: Westminster Press, 1953; also available in paperback), pp. 161–202. The Greek text, with translation by Kirsopp Lake, is conveniently available in Lake's edition of *The Apostolic Fathers* (Loeb Classical Library; London: Heinemann; Cambridge, Mass.: Harvard University Press, 1952). There are excellent notes and critical comments in Robert A. Kraft, *Barnabas and the Didache*, vol. 3 of *The Apostolic Fathers*, ed. by Robert M. Grant (New York, Toronto, and London: Thomas Nelson & Sons, 1965).

9. Trans. by Robert A. Kraft (see previous note).

10. Bentley Layton, "The Sources, Date and Transmission of *Didache* 1.3b–2.1," *Harvard Theological Review* 61 (1968), 343–383.

11. Layton has meticulously reconstructed his procedure, in the article named in the previous note.

12. For examples and discussion of "retelling" and paraphrase of biblical narratives and codes in Jewish communities, see James Kugel and Rowan

A. Greer, *Early Biblical Interpretation* (Library of Early Christianity; Philadelphia: Westminster Press, 1986), chs. 4 and 5.

13. Layton, pp. 348–349, argues persuasively that a series of scribal mistakes converted this into the apparently cynical remark found in the received text, "You could not (get it back anyway)."

14. See Rule of the Community (1QS) 5.24–6.1.

15. Quotations from Irenaeus, *Against Heresies,* are from the translation by Alexander Roberts and James Donaldson, eds., *The Ante-Nicene Fathers,* vol. 1 (Grand Rapids: Wm. B. Eerdmans Publishing Co., 1950; original American edition, 1885; Edinburgh edition, 1868). The chapter and section numbers are those of Massuet's edition of the text (rather than Harvey's).

16. J. Armitage Robinson, ed. and trans., *St. Irenaeus, The Demonstration of the Apostolic Preaching* (London: S.P.C.K., 1920). In what follows, quotations from the *Proof* are from the translation by Joseph P. Smith, *St. Irenaeus, Proof of the Apostolic Preaching* (Ancient Christian Writers, 16; Westminster, Md.: Newman Press; London: Longmans, Green, 1952). Sometimes, as here, I have used Robinson's translation. The *Proof* survives only in a single manuscript and some small fragments of a sixth-century Armenian translation from the Greek.

17. See the Introduction above and Geertz's famous essay, quoted there, "Ethos, World-View, and the Analysis of Sacred Symbols," *Antioch Review* 17 (1957–58), 421–437; reprinted in his *The Interpretation of Cultures* (New York: Basic Books, 1973), pp. 126–141.

18. Richardson, *Early Christian Fathers,* p. 352.

19. For a further discussion of early Christian reading of scripture and of Irenaeus' place in it, see the final two chapters of Kugel-Greer, *Early Biblical Interpretation* (see note 12 of this chapter).

Suggestions
for Further Reading

The notes have referred to many useful studies, whose names are not repeated here. For a survey of recent literature, see Pheme Perkins, "New Testament Ethics: Questions and Contexts," *Religious Studies Review* 10/4 (1984), 321–327. The following selection represents a diversity of viewpoints in ethics and in New Testament studies, in accessible English-language books.

Deidun, Thomas J. *New Covenant Morality in Paul.* Analecta Biblica, 89. Rome: Biblical Institute Press, 1981.

Fiorenza, Elisabeth Schüssler. *In Memory of Her: A Feminist Theological Reconstruction of Christian Origins.* New York: Crossroad Publishing Co., 1983.

Fuller, Reginald H., et al. *Essays on the Love Command.* Philadelphia: Fortress Press, 1978.

Furnish, Victor P. *Theology and Ethics in Paul.* Nashville and New York: Abingdon Press, 1968.

———. *The Love Command in the New Testament.* Nashville and New York: Abingdon Press, 1972.

Hauerwas, Stanley. *The Peaceable Kingdom: A Primer in Christian Ethics.* Notre Dame and London: University of Notre Dame Press, 1983.

Hengel, Martin. *Property and Riches in the Early Church: Aspects of a Social History of Early Christianity.* Philadelphia: Fortress Press, 1975.

Johnson, Luke T. *Sharing Possessions: Mandate and Symbol of Faith.* Philadelphia: Fortress Press, 1981.

Lohfink, Gerhard. *Jesus and Community: The Social Dimension of Christian Faith.* Philadelphia: Fortress Press; New York and Ramsey, N.J.: Paulist Press, 1984.

MacIntyre, Alasdair. *After Virtue: A Study in Moral Theory.* 2nd ed. Notre Dame and London: University of Notre Dame Press, 1984.

Mott, Stephen Charles. *Biblical Ethics and Social Change.* New York and Oxford: Oxford University Press, 1982.

Ogletree, Thomas. *The Use of the Bible in Christian Ethics.* Philadelphia: Fortress Press, 1983.

Perkins, Pheme. *Love Commands in the New Testament.* New York and Ramsey, N.J.: Paulist Press, 1982.

Rist, John M. *Human Value: A Study in Ancient Philosophical Ethics.* Philosophia Antiqua, 40. Leiden: E. J. Brill, 1982.

Schnackenburg, Rudolf. *The Moral Teaching of the New Testament.* London: Burns & Oates, 1965.

Verhey, Allen. *The Great Reversal: Ethics and the New Testament.* Grand Rapids: Wm. B. Eerdmans Publishing Co., 1984.

Williams, Bernard. *Ethics and the Limits of Philosophy.* Cambridge, Mass.: Harvard University Press, 1985.

Yoder, John Howard. *The Priestly Kingdom: Social Ethics as Gospel.* Notre Dame: University of Notre Dame Press, 1985.

Index of Selected Subjects

Index of New Testament Passages